DISCOVER HAPPINESS:

HOW TO REINVENT YOURSELF AND FIND YOUR PURPOSE

FRANKIE COTTO

LEGAL DISCLAIMER AND TERMS OF USE

The author has aimed to present the most complete and accurate content possible; however, we cannot provide any guarantees due to the rapid changes in the world we live in. Although every effort was made to verify the information provided here, the author is not responsible for any errors, omissions, or contradictions subject to interpretation. "Discover Happiness: How to Reinvent Yourself and Find Your Purpose" is a book written solely as a source of inspiration and information. The content should not be used as a substitute for evaluations and/or recommendations from your doctor, nutritionist, financial professional, or qualified healthcare provider. You should consult your indicated professional before starting this or any changes presented as information related to health, work, or financial matters.

DEDICATION

I want to dedicate this book first and foremost to my Lord Jesus Christ, who, despite the difficult times I have had to go through, has never abandoned me.

To my friend, counselor, confident, and wife Jeany, who has been my companion on this journey for the past 43 years and counting. Thank you for granting me the time and space to work on this project.

To my children, Jessenia and her husband Reinaldo Cintrón, Josué, as well as my grandchildren Sarah and Lucas; you are a great inspiration to me.

I can't leave out my sister-in-law, Elena Franqui, and her husband, Ronald Sánchez. They opened their home to help us through the transition when we arrived from Puerto Rico after Hurricane Maria. Thanks to them, we were able to begin a new phase of our lives. Their kindness is unforgettable.

Lastly, I dedicate this to all those who have suffered the pain of failure, betrayal, loss, and continue with the desire to succeed in life, and seek inspiration to overcome. I hope this can give you the encouragement and motivation to rise up and keep fighting. Don't give up!

SPECIAL THANKS AND ACKNOWLEDGMENTS

I would like to express my sincere gratitude to several individuals who have significantly influenced and contributed to the creation of this book.

To ***Rashika Gupta***, for her impeccable editing and translation of the book. You arrived at just the right moment after many attempts, and your work has been essential.

Jacob Brown, your dedication and effort have not gone unnoticed. I greatly appreciate your honesty, integrity, and collaboration; without your intervention, this book would not have been possible.

To ***Disney*** and all those who lent me a hand in my transition to Florida after Hurricane Maria. Your unconditional support and the opportunity to be part of such a vibrant community not only helped me rebuild my life, but also served as validation for this book. I am eternally grateful for the warmth and sense of belonging they gave me at such a crucial time.

To ***Dean Graziosi*** and ***Tony Robbins***, whom I have followed for over 20 years. Although I have not yet had the pleasure of meeting them in person, their work has been a mainstay for me. Ironically, I met Tony in the same way and under the same circumstances as Dean, when the internet did not yet exist. Perhaps that is why I resonate so much with your coaching. Both of you have been a great source of inspiration, and I am deeply grateful for your mentorship.

To Pastor ***Jorge Cotto***, who, in addition to being my brother, is my spiritual guide. His advice and insights have helped me at critical crossroads. Your honest answers and advice always came at the right time.

To my pastor ***Tim Goad*** and the G5 church in Florida, who welcomed us with love during difficult times, making us feel at home. I am eternally grateful.

TABLE OF CONTENTS

INTRODUCTION

"Life is never made unbearable by circumstances, but only by lack of meaning and purpose."

Viktor Frankl

The meeting was about to begin. I was the vice president and security director at a bank, and at that moment, I was co-leading a task force composed of security directors from all the banks in Puerto Rico, the FBI, the Secret Service, State Police, Postal Inspectors, among others. The group had been organized by the Puerto Rico Bankers Association to tackle a wave of frauds and robberies targeting banks and consumers, which was growing rapidly. This effort aimed to alleviate and prevent frauds that sometimes started at one bank and were repeated at others by the same individual or organization.

The San Juan Star B-3

Bankers' anti-fraud group asks for consumers' help

BY JOSE ALVARADO VEGA

An anti-fraud working group of bankers and commonwealth and federal law enforcement officials urged consumers to keep an eye out for and report cases of identity theft.

"We are asking consumers to be careful when using their credit and debit cards and help us with information so we can build up cases that we can take to court," Arturo Carrión, executive director of the Puerto Rico Bankers Association, said in a press conference Wednesday in Hato Rey.

Carrión was accompanied by bank executives and officials from the Police Department, FBI and U.S. Postal Inspection Service, which form part of the association's anti-fraud working group. The group, established in November 2002, collects and cross-checks information from banks and shares it with different commonwealth and federal law-enforcement agencies, Carrión said. Members meet every two weeks.

The group is working to prevent and obtain prosecutions for cases involving identity theft, check fraud, credit and debit card fraud, mortgage fraud and Web fraud.

Identity theft is generally perpetrated to facilitate other crimes, such as credit card fraud, check fraud or mortgage fraud, officials said at the press conference.

Fraud involving credit and debit cards cost banks in Puerto Rico about $30 million last year, Carrión said. Losses that result from debit cards and credit cards issued from banks are absorbed by the banks themselves, he added.

"Information gathered by this group has led to arrests and prosecutions," he said.

Héctor Torres, vice president of security at Banco Popular and chairman of the Bankers Association security committee, said that the group helped to crack a recent case.

Torres said a gang operated a scheme in which cashiers would swap customers' credit cards in a separate machine to pick up access information, in a process called skimming.

"This was an extremely organized group, but our efforts resulted in multiple arrests and broke up the ring," he said. "When credit card or debit card fraud is committed, it is not isolated; it spreads to other banks and businesses."

The group is also lobbying the legislature to pass anti-fraud bills. While the Senate has approved legislation making financial fraud a crime in Puerto Rico, the House has stalled in considering the bills, Carrión said.

The Legislature originally wanted to include fraud legislation in

Please see "BANKERS," Page B-8

From left, J.R. Luareano, U.S. Postal Inspector; Angel F. Cotto, vice president of BankTrust; Juan B. De La Cruz, vice president of Doral Financial; Bankers Association Executive Director Arturo Carrión and Banco Popular's Vice President for Security Héctor Torres.

Minutes before starting, I looked around the long conference table of about 20 people, and that's when an unexpected and interesting conversation began in my mind. I started asking myself, "How did I get here? I see more qualified people, but why me?" I was the only one present who had never belonged to the armed forces or any law enforcement agency or security-related field. Yet, I found myself participating in an inter-agency effort with people of great caliber and experience representing their respective banks or law enforcement agencies.

I even remembered the moment when I had left university studies feeling confused. While at my parents' house, a family friend who attended the same church as us asked my dad if I wasn't studying. Dad told him, and as he was leaving, he told me to go to the bank where he worked to fill out a job application.

The next morning, I went, and that very day, they hired me. As you read through the book, I want you to identify the importance of having a healthy relationship with *whomever* you have chosen as your supreme being. Many times, I had asked myself, "What would have happened to my life if he hadn't gone to visit my dad, or if I hadn't been at home at that exact time?" I've discovered that there is a very powerful spiritual force that needs to be aligned with the knowledge of human behavior, and you will begin to discover this as you immerse yourself in the content of the book.

Returning to the moment of the meeting, I can't tell you that it was an audible voice, but I felt words in my conversation that sounded like this: "You dreamed it, you asked for it, you insisted, and I granted it." My eyes welled up, and I felt deeply moved and grateful. It was a very profound spiritual experience, and it led my mind to remember my beginnings, longings, and professional desires. Something I wanted initially but didn't know how to obtain.

Through the pages of this book, I will take you on a journey full of surprises, facts, and results that may not have a logical explanation for you, and you may interpret it as a miracle or perhaps as coincidence. However, it will motivate you to re-evaluate the way you have lived and what you have achieved so far. I will invite you to step out of the box of comfort or fear that you've been living in until now and that has prevented you from living the life you were designed for.

Before continuing, allow me to welcome you to a journey of transformation and self-discovery. Reinventing oneself doesn't necessarily mean changing jobs or careers. It's about recognizing how to be happy regardless of circumstances and from there, discovering your life's purpose and reinventing yourself to fulfill it.

I've learned that when we find a way to be happier, we become the best version of ourselves. This leads us to be better partners, employees, entrepreneurs, and, in the end, stable individuals capable of achieving anything we set our minds to.

Let me share with you a personal experience that changed my life. For many years, I focused on my professional career, seeking progress and success. However, in the process, I neglected my health. My body was aging prematurely, and when I sought motivation to change, many around me told me it was normal. Not only that, but they were very emphatic in saying that I should wait until I was 40, as that's when the pains would start.

Have you noticed that when you want to do something with your life, you seek help or support, but no one seems to understand you? Everyone knows about the topic, whatever it may be, but they've never really tried or done it, and they don't seem to want anyone to achieve what they couldn't. Nevertheless, I resisted accepting that as my fate. I embarked on a quest to recover my health and rejuvenate my body.

It wasn't an easy task. Back then, there were no resources like YouTube or Google to guide me. I had been a researcher, so I applied that knowledge in my desperate search. Along the way, I began doing the same things I had done when I was younger, things you've probably also tried. Running, playing basketball, riding a bicycle, and even aerobics. Eating lettuce and tomatoes, the diets I found in bodybuilding magazines, among other attempts, but nothing worked.

I had been trying different methods for a few months, without achieving the desired result when a great opportunity arose. There's a saying that goes, *"When the student is ready, the teacher appears."* After several failed attempts, I was invited to get certified as a personal trainer. This was the key that transformed my life. Not only did I transform my own body, but I also witnessed wonders in the lives of the people I helped.

Although I continued working at the bank, in my free time, I trained people at my house. That's when the transformation began, not only because they improved their health, but also because their mood elevated, and mine changed as well. I became so passionate about what was happening that I decided this would be part of my plan when I retired. What I didn't know was that a few years later, something I will tell you later, that job would be my only source of income. Today, at 64 years old, I continue enjoying a healthy body thanks to that decision.

This experience not only gave me a new career, but it also taught me the power of reinvention and the importance of following our passions to serve others. By placing service as our priority, we not only find purpose and satisfaction, but we also create a positive impact in the lives of others. I use a saying that goes: *"Fight, insist, and you will succeed."* From the moment we are born, we begin to fight for our space in this world. You go to school, then university or work, they tell you to get married and have a nice family, you do it, you start working in a place you don't like and doing something you don't enjoy. Then, you get frustrated and ask yourself, is this all there is in life?

Oh, maybe you're doing very well financially, you have a wonderful family, and you're pleased with your achievement, but still, you feel empty and desire more from life, but you don't know what and even less how to achieve it. However, at the first setback, others give up with the deceptions created by others, incorrect beliefs, many giving up without achieving their dream or fulfilling their purpose. A minority decides to insist, and that's when the miracle happens.

At 40, I insisted and was able to reinvent myself despite the negative predictions others prophesied for me, until I found the map to transform my body. This experience made me passionate about fitness and led me to open a gym, which I also thought was my purpose. It was a huge investment of time, effort, and money, but the 2008 economic recession changed all my plans. I lost everything, including my job at the bank where I worked. At 50, I found myself having to start over. It was not easy to accept, to disappoint people who trusted and believed in you, especially when what you're trying to do is genuine and in good faith.

Frustrated and hurt but not defeated, I began to explore new opportunities. I leaned on my skills and experiences and started a new career as a personal trainer. Despite my age, my body and energy rejuvenated, which led me to write my first book, "Your Best Body At Any Age," followed by "Your Well-Being Is A Priority." These books opened doors for public speaking and sharing my vision of well-being.

However, life shook me again when Hurricane Maria destroyed the hopes I had in Puerto Rico. My family and I moved to Florida, and just when I was beginning to lift my head, my wife suffered a serious accident. I decided to put my projects on hold for three years to care for her, but I never gave up my search for happiness.

Working at Disney World, "the happiest place on earth," I saw how my enthusiasm impacted others. It was then that my mission to bring joy, combined with other experiences, pushed me to change my environment.

Inspired by my experiences, along with courses and readings on happiness, I wanted to help others find their well-being. I combined my knowledge with my experience to create contingency programs in banks, to face challenges and maintain joy. Through this book, I want to guide you in an entertaining and educational way to prepare your emotions and strengthen your happiness. You will learn events from my life that I had not made public. I want my mistakes to become your lessons; together, we can transform adversity into growth. In my experience, being happy is the formula to open new opportunities in any area of life. Before reinventing yourself for money, seek happiness in every moment.

The book is divided into two parts. We will begin by exploring happiness as an essential pillar of our lives, discovering its many facets and how to cultivate it in our day-to-day lives. However, true satisfaction doesn't end in achieving happiness, it multiplies when we venture to reinvent ourselves, a process that leads us to rediscover our deepest passions and purposes.

As Buddha rightly states, *"Your work is to discover your work, and then give your heart to it."* With this sense of adventure, in the second part, we will embark on this journey of personal transformation. Modern life presents us with countless opportunities for this change, and the key lies in serving others with what truly excites us.

It is this spirit of reinvention focused on service that I want to explore with you in the second part of this book. Your mission, if you choose to accept it, is to start seeing life from a new perspective, recognize your strengths and weaknesses, and discover how you can reinvent yourself to serve. We will use the foundations of happiness you have already learned and apply them to design a life that not only gives you personal satisfaction but also allows you to serve as an inspiration and help to others.

Reinvention is not abandoning who you are, but embracing who you are destined to be. Reinventing yourself does not mean starting from scratch or changing everything overnight; rather, it is an act of constant evolution. We leverage what we already are, our experiences, and learnings to build an improved version of ourselves. Every step toward reinvention is an opportunity to align ourselves more with our true desires and potential.

As we move forward in this reinvention journey, it is essential to understand that true change comes with purpose and authenticity. In the second part, I will explain practical methods and deep strategies that will help you find your true passion, define your purpose, and plan each step toward a life full of meaning and service. Get ready to discover valuable tools and reflective exercises that will accompany you through each stage of this exciting personal reinvention journey.

How did I come to these conclusions and strategies? When I worked in banks, some of my responsibilities were investigations and preparing business continuity plans. In other words, I had to have an alternative plan in case of a disaster, so the bank could keep its vital processes until the worst part of the emergency passed. Then, we had to have the steps ready to restore the operation. Have you ever wondered how you could transform adversity into an opportunity? Are you an insecure person who gets blocked when a problem is in front of you?

While going through all the difficulties in my path, I began to integrate research concepts, adapting them to my personal life to maintain my progress. I created alternative plans for my family and was able to overcome adversity when it arose. I remember when I lost everything; I reviewed my plan to find income alternatives. Becoming a security consultant was the first thing I considered, but the crisis at that time prevented it from materializing.

Another option was to become a personal trainer. Through contacts, I found a temporary opportunity while looking for more alternatives. Exploring my abilities, I realized that I knew how to write, speak in public, and manage. Thus, I continued my progress in relatively new fields that allowed me to reinvent myself as a writer, speaker, and coach.

Having your skills and experience written down allows you to put them into practice quickly. Without a plan, facing emergencies can cloud your vision and make decision-making difficult. Additionally, I discovered the importance of maintaining a positive attitude: smiling at life and moving forward with perseverance, an attitude crucial to overcoming challenges.

In this book, I will guide you to have clarity and focus in adverse times. Not only that, but I will also show you how to monetize your passion and share your purpose with others, to live a fulfilling life. Get ready to transform your curiosity and knowledge into a new beginning full of opportunities.

All this information comes from a careful selection of books, learnings from mentors and coaches, experiences, and my investment of time and money. My goal is for this knowledge to enrich your life significantly, just as it did mine.

Thank you for joining this journey. I am here with you every step of the way, ready to support you. If you're ready, turn the page and let's start the most important journey of your life.

CHAPTER 1:
UNDERSTANDING HAPPINESS

"The secret of happiness is not doing what you want all the time, but wanting all the time what you do."

Leo Tolstoy

This lady came up to me and, as I usually do, I asked with a smile I can't avoid: "Hello, how are you ma'am?" In a somewhat hostile and bad-tempered tone or as if out of obligation, she replied: "I'm fine, and you?" I smiled again and replied: "Happy to be alive." She paused, stopped what she was doing, and looked me straight in the eyes, saying: "You have no idea what you've done. I came here upset because I had to walk too much, it's hot, and I'm tired."

"However, I am a cancer survivor, and I should have your attitude. Thank you for changing my day." She asked if she could give me a hug, and I said: "Of course." We hugged, and then she left with a huge smile and a very different attitude than when she arrived. That was a key and important moment in which I validated what I had already been suspecting about my life's purpose, which I will reveal to you.

In this chapter, I want you to explore for yourself the importance of understanding happiness. Mastering this principle is crucial to living a full and authentic life. Happiness is not just for weekends, nor is it achieved when you buy a new car or go on vacation. It is a reality backed by science.

What is Happiness?

Before embarking on a journey toward personal and/or professional reinvention, it is vital to learn to be happy first. This understanding will allow you to control stress, maintain focus, and build a solid foundation for any change you choose to undertake.

True happiness does not reside in a new car, a big house, or a hefty bank account. Believe me, I've been in those positions, and what kept me going when I lost everything was learning to be content in every circumstance. Genuine happiness is an inner state, influenced by our mindset, the relationships we cultivate, and the small daily practices that contribute to our well-being.

My inner dialogue was crucial. I went from having a company-paid car to riding a bike due to financial difficulties. That forced change taught me that, even though my mind tried to deceive me, I could divert negative thoughts and begin to enjoy the bike ride. This experience strengthened my mind and spirit and revealed the power of personal transformation.

When you stop fighting against life's tough events and obstacles, you begin to see it differently. You start to see opportunities instead of obstacles, and miracles begin to happen.

Inspirational Stories

Consider figures like:

- Steve Jobs: Fired from Apple, he founded NeXT and bought Pixar, before returning triumphantly to Apple and revolutionizing modern technology.

- J.K. Rowling: From a single mother living on social assistance to one of the most successful authors, proving that perseverance conquers adversity.

- Walt Disney: Fired for "lack of imagination," he created an entertainment empire, including the iconic Mickey Mouse.

These stories should inspire you to open your mind and change your reality. Contrary to what others think, I believe you were born to be happy, offering your talents in the service of what you are passionate about. The Bible says in Romans 15:13, "And the God of hope fill you with all joy and peace in believing."

Although this book is not about talking to you about any particular religion, I must reaffirm my experience in the light of my faith. I respect yours and only intend for you to also evaluate how you have lived and the results obtained. In the end, you will have a clearer vision of the changes, if any, that you need to make to achieve happiness and reinvent yourself in a powerful way. In the second part of the book, I will teach you how to do this.

Clarifying Material Happiness

It is not just about money, but about fulfilling our life's mission. Studies show that after meeting basic needs; money has little impact on happiness. Relentlessly pursuing material goods can hide a life of dissatisfaction, which is definitely not what I want for you.

The Science of Happiness

Studies from Harvard University and others suggest that our relationships and internal perceptions are key to well-being. 40% of our happiness is under our control, and adopting positive habits can transform our lives.

Happiness is a state that has intrigued both scientists and spiritual leaders. While science offers theories on neurotransmitters and the influence of the environment on our well-being, Christian perspectives offer a deeper and more reflective view. From the teachings of the Beatitudes, where we are revealed that true happiness comes from living in peace, being humble and merciful, to the fruits of the Spirit such as love, joy, and peace, we discover that happiness is not just a passing feeling but a state of fulfillment and divine grace.

Just as it reflects the joy of serving others, Christianity guides us to find happiness by being valuable to others. In hope and faith lies the strength to face daily challenges, while spiritual contentment teaches us to appreciate what we have and be grateful for the blessings in our life. By integrating these elements into our daily experience, we gain a more complete understanding of happiness, transcending the limits of the material and finding a higher purpose.

Inspirational Story: A Transformational Change

Consider the story of Megan, a successful executive who felt empty despite having everything socially considered essential for happiness. She began practicing daily gratitude and investing in her personal relationships, which gave her genuine happiness. Her personal transformation was not about her career, but about finding joy in the everyday.

And if you want more depth, consider my own case, I was a young man who didn't know what to study. I even gave up before finishing my first year of college. However, in a way that I interpret as miraculous, I became a bank vice president, lived experiences I never thought I would have, and continue to have. Through what we have left to share, you will discover why I think this way.

At one point, despite the experiences and achievements I had gained miraculously, I dared to ask something that deep inside I had thought but had never had the courage to question. The question was this: "Why do I believe in God? Is it because my parents taught me? I don't know if this has happened to you, that you've had many questions, but you don't dare ask them, not even question them or talk about them because you think you'll sin or offend someone?"

There are moments when you have to take the courage you don't have and question. By doing so, you will receive liberation, live in peace, and see the path to your life's purpose more clearly. Simply because things are no longer in the hands of another person, but because you freely establish a direct line with your Creator, without intermediaries or people trying to impose their own criteria on you. When we reach the second part where we will talk about reinvention, you will better understand what I mean. But you must have the right knowledge so you can decide for yourself in the proper way.

Various Scientific Approaches

- Professor of Psychology and director of "Yale's Comparative Cognition Laboratory," Lauri Santos has extensively researched the science of happiness. Through her course "The Science of Well-Being," Santos offers strategies to increase well-being through practices such as gratitude and meditation.

- Arthur Brooks a renowned academic and author, analyzes happiness from socio-economic and cultural perspectives. In his book *The Art of Happiness,* Brooks emphasizes the importance of human connections and life purpose in achieving true happiness.

- A professor of positive psychology at Harvard, Tal Ben-Shahar promotes happiness through small daily acts. He highlights how kindness, gratitude, and a positive mindset significantly contribute to personal well-being.

Self-Assessment Exercise

- Write your own definition of happiness and assess if you accept the challenge to be happier than you are today.

NOTES

CHAPTER 2:
SELF-KNOWLEDGE AND AUTHENTICITY

"Knowing yourself is the beginning of all wisdom."
Aristotle

The Importance of Self-Knowledge

At a certain point in my professional career, I found myself questioning if this was all the meaning my life would have. I worked so hard to earn the title I had longed for since I began working in banks. Yet, I felt that something was missing. There was a deep restlessness within me that urged me to seek a sense of greater meaning.

The problem was that I didn't know how to search for it or even what it was. My mind kept asking questions and answering them by itself. I don't know if you've ever experienced this—trying to find answers but feeling too scared or embarrassed to confess them or share them.

I journeyed countless times through the tunnel of time—my history, my beginnings—and I kept reaching the same point: How did I get here? My mind took me back to a crucial moment in my life when I was at a crossroads, trying to decide which path to take in my professional career. It was 1978, and I had to decide what I would do after graduating high school. At my counselor's suggestion, I took a career aptitude test that led me to the fields of psychology or sociology.

But the teacher crushed that spark of light and hope when he told me those professionals were unemployed and to forget about it. I remember my sense of frustration. So, my initial desire shifted, and I now wanted to enlist in the army and eventually become a federal agent. However, concerns and warnings from my mother and other family members made me second-guess myself.

While their intentions were good, they planted fears and insecurities in me, convincing me to go to college and pursue a career I knew nothing about. Have you ever noticed that when you want to do something with your life, which is *yours*, everyone has an opinion? Everyone thinks they know what's good for you, what you should do, and even how you should do it. "Study something where you can make a lot of money, gain prestige, and work in air conditioning." "Something where you wear a suit and tie or a white coat." Anything but "Do something that makes you happy, aligns with your interests, values, talents, and abilities." This happened to me, and it was a significant realization that illuminated my existence.

Although I support scientific evidence when making decisions and achieving desired outcomes, I cannot overlook the power of spiritual miracles. Let me explain what I mean. Although I didn't know what to study after high school, as a young, indecisive, introverted, and insecure person, my relationship with God was very close. I believe the success I had was due to Him. You might ask how I became a vice president after describing my personality this way. Let me call it a miracle.

To make a long story short, in 1986, I decided to venture to the United States in search of better opportunities. However, things didn't go as expected, and I decided to return to Puerto Rico. When I came back from Miami to start over in 1989, I began working at a very small bank with a great growth plan. As that expansion phase started, the workload piled up to the point that it became too much for the existing employees. To make matters worse, the person in charge of the department didn't give it much attention. I was working seven days a week, and my wife would bring the kids to the bank so I could see them.

My emotional health started to decline, and I requested a meeting with the Human Resources office. The director suggested I request a transfer, which I did. The very day I was set to start, I was informed that there was a termination order against me. Everything I had reported as needing attention had spiraled out of control, and I was blamed for the department's inefficiency.

However, I was given a chance to search for a discrepancy in the Bank that amounted to $2 million. They gave me a folding table and piled a huge stack of reports on it. Colleagues who knew what was happening encouraged me not to let them humiliate me that way, to protest, or even quit. In my mind, an intense debate began.

On one side was the option to leave, while on the other was the decision to search for and resolve the problem. I chose the second option. Two months later, the bank bought another one, and I was put in charge of transitioning and relocating operations. Once that was done, I returned to my folding table to look for the remaining $200,000 missing. That morning, the president called me into his office, and after mentioning the name of the person who had been my boss, he ended by saying that he was no longer with the bank and that if I did my job well, in three months, I would be made vice president.

I left the office wanting to shout, laugh, and dance. However, as I walked toward the exit, my mind reminded me that half of the responsibilities I was assuming, I had never done before. Doubt began to creep in, but I stopped the conversation in my head, knowing that if God had opened the door, He would help me, and indeed, He did. For me, it was a powerful miracle and a lesson that when you believe, anything can happen.

Self-Knowledge is the foundation of an authentic and happy life. Brown and Ryan, two researchers who have worked extensively in the field of Psychology, especially in areas related to self-knowledge, mindfulness, and psychological well-being, have delved deeply into this topic. A study they conducted suggests that a higher level of self-knowledge and mindfulness is associated with increased satisfaction and overall well-being.

Furthermore, authenticity is linked to less stress and a greater ability to face challenges. Authentic people are more likely to establish and maintain healthy relationships, which is essential for achieving happiness.

This is why I believe it is extremely important to engage in a self-knowledge exercise that helps you understand what you truly want. Believe me, you will feel more relaxed and much happier than you do now. Later on, you'll do a simple exercise that will allow you to better understand this self-discovery, which is so important for you and your relationship with your creator.

Transformation

Let me share a story that is very close to my heart—mine. As you know, I am a transformation and well-being coach. My own journey into self-knowledge began when I went through a personal crisis. Despite having a successful career, I felt an emptiness I couldn't ignore. I decided to take a step back and explore my true values and passions.

As I embarked on this internal adventure, I discovered that my true passion was helping others find their happiness and reinvent themselves. This authenticity has provided me with a joy and purpose that I never could have imagined. By sharing my story, I hope to inspire others to embark on their own journeys of self-discovery.

Scientific Approaches

The research by Kernis and Goldman on authenticity suggests that being true to oneself leads to a richer and more meaningful life. Being authentic means living consistently with your values and beliefs, even in the face of difficulties.

Alex M. Wood and his team have studied how authenticity is related to psychological well-being. They have found that being authentic is associated with higher self-esteem, life satisfaction, and lower anxiety and depression. Through various methodologies, including long-term and single-moment studies, they have demonstrated that acting authentically greatly improves emotional and mental health. They suggest that fostering authenticity could be an effective strategy to improve mental health.

Michael H. Kernis and Brian M. Goldman have conducted important work on what it means to be authentic in psychology. They say that being authentic means being sincere with oneself and others. This includes knowing oneself well, thinking justly, acting according to our true intentions, and maintaining good relationships. They created the "Authenticity Inventory," a tool that measures these aspects and has been very useful in understanding how authenticity improves our happiness and personal satisfaction.

Edward L. Deci and Richard M. Ryan, known for their self-determination theory, have also explored authenticity. In their theory, authenticity is seen as a basic psychological need that promotes personal growth and well-being. They argue that being authentic—acting in accordance with internal values and needs—is crucial for psychological health and personal fulfillment.

Their research shows that environments that support autonomy, competence, and social relationships promote a stronger sense of authenticity and, consequently, higher levels of well-being.

It is time for you to discover your true authenticity. Why you are here in this world and, most importantly, how to be happy while living your life's mission. Reinvention doesn't just mean changing jobs, so don't be afraid.

You can reinvent yourself exactly where you are, doing something that partially excites you, even in your free time. Before becoming who I am today, I served as a volunteer youth counselor, and believe me, it brought me moments I still cherish in my heart.

Self-Discovery and Authenticity Exercise

Objective: Reflect on your values and identity. This step is vital because once you have clarity, you avoid internal conflicts that will steal your happiness, peace, and productivity.

Instructions:

- Sit in a quiet place where you feel comfortable and free from distractions.
- Take three deep breaths to relax and center yourself.
- Answer the following questions sincerely without overthinking:
    - What activities do I enjoy in my free time?
    - When do I feel most authentic and at peace with myself?
    - What values are most important to me and why?
    - What has been one of the happiest moments of my life, and what made it special?
    - If you could give advice to your younger self from five, ten or twenty years ago, what would you say?
- Read what you've written and look for recurring patterns or themes. Highlight or underline the words or phrases that resonate most with you.
- Choose one activity or value that stands out and find a way to integrate it more into your daily life.

When we get to reinvention, we'll talk more about how you can monetize your passion and/or purpose, if that's your desire.

NOTES

CHAPTER 3: DAILY PRACTICES TO CULTIVATE HAPPINESS

"Son, life is short. Be joyful, be happy, and make someone smile."

Angel F. Cotto, my dad

The Importance of Small Routines

My dad was a very cheerful man who spent his time telling jokes and making people laugh. Even in the hospital, while battling terminal cancer, he joked with every nurse and doctor who entered his room. He never asked why he was there or what he was suffering from; he simply smiled and played his usual pranks. One week before closing his eyes to this world, after a joke, he looked at me and said, "Son, life is short. Be joyful, be happy, and make someone smile."

Although I considered myself a happy person up until that moment, that experience made me want to be even happier and commit to making others smile. Gratitude became and continues to be an essential part of my life because I discovered that it is impossible to be happy without feeling grateful for life. That's why I adopted the response you may already know to the common question people ask: "How are you?" My answer is, "Happy to be alive."

On one occasion, an executive asked me, "How are you, Frankie?" I replied with a big smile and enthusiasm, "Happy to be alive." He looked at me and said, "I wish I had your energy and happiness." Without hesitation, I responded: "When you lose everything you worked hard for with honesty and sacrifice, you learn to value what you have, no matter how small it may be, and you are grateful for how fortunate you are to be alive." What he—and many others—did not know was that I had been a bank vice president, the owner of my own business, and at the peak of my career when life surprised me not once but multiple times by taking it all away.

What I want you to remember is that through gratitude, we can realize how fortunate we are. The control you have over your thoughts will positively or negatively impact your day. You don't need to wait for a vacation, a party, or buying something you like to experience the joy of living. The problem lies in focusing on what we don't have instead of appreciating what we do, no matter how little or small it may be.

What I want you to understand is that happiness is not a destination; it's a journey built through daily practices and habits. In studies conducted by the University of California, psychologist Sonja Lyubomirsky found that everyday activities like gratitude, regular exercise, and meditation can significantly increase our happiness.

Inspiring Story: The Power of Gratitude

Let's take the example of Juan, a businessman who was always stressed and overwhelmed. He decided to start a gratitude journal, writing three things he was thankful for each day. Over time, this simple practice helped him change his perspective and value the small moments in life. Juan not only improved his mood but also strengthened his relationships and work performance.

Scientific Approaches

You should know that the practice of gratitude has been supported by numerous studies. A study by Emmons and McCullough found that people who keep a gratitude journal experience greater emotional well-being and fewer symptoms of depression.

Meditation and mindfulness also play a crucial role in happiness. The *Journal of Personality and Social Psychology* published a study showing that meditation can increase life satisfaction and reduce stress.

When you have faith in something greater than ourselves—whether it's a spiritual force, divine power, or a larger purpose—

it can profoundly impact our happiness and well-being. Research in the field of psychology has shown that people with spiritual or religious beliefs often report higher levels of life satisfaction.

This positive relationship between faith and happiness can be explained in several ways:

1. **Faith provides a sense of purpose and meaning in life.** When people believe in something larger than themselves, they can find deeper purpose and a reason to overcome daily challenges.

2. **Faith offers comfort and hope in times of adversity.** Spiritual and religious beliefs can provide an inner source of strength and stress reduction, helping individuals better cope with difficulties and tragedies.

3. **Faith fosters a sense of community and connection.** Religious and spiritual practices often involve participating in groups and community activities that strengthen social relationships and mutual support, both crucial factors for happiness.

4. **Faith promotes values such as gratitude, compassion, and forgiveness,** which are associated with greater emotional well-being.

A clarification I want to highlight is the difference between meditation and prayer. In my opinion, they are separate yet very similar things. Prayer is the medium through which you communicate with that supreme being in whom you believe, which in my case, as I've mentioned, is God. Meditation is a practice that controls your mind and emotions, keeping them in check. There are many methods and styles—find the one that works best for you.

Daily Gratitude and Reflection Exercise:

1. Dedicate 5–10 Minutes Every Morning:

    - **Reflect on Gratitude:** When you wake up, think of three things you are grateful for. These can be simple joys like a good night's sleep, a hug from a loved one, or the aroma of morning coffee.

2. Write Down Your Thoughts:

    - **Gratitude Journal:** Keep a journal to record the three things you're grateful for each day. Store it in an easily accessible spot so you can revisit and reflect on your entries.

3. Set a Daily Intention:

    - **Positive Focus:** Before starting your day, establish a positive intention, such as: *"Today, I will find moments of joy"* or *"I will face challenges with calm and optimism."*

4. Practice Meditation or Mindful Breathing:

    - **Calm Your Mind:** Spend a few minutes meditating or practicing mindful breathing to set a peaceful and positive tone for your day.

5. Evening Reflection:

    - **Celebrate Successes:** At the end of the day, take a few minutes to reflect on what went well and what you learned. Write down three things that made you happy during the day.

6. Acts of Kindness:

    - **Spread Positivity:** Aim to perform one act of kindness each day, no matter how small. It could be as simple as smiling at someone or helping a coworker.

The "MVP" System for Mindset and Happiness:

I incorporate and teach these practices in my coaching programs under the "MVP" system:

- **M - Meditate daily:** Spend at least 5 minutes meditating each day.
- **V - Visualize the life you desire:** Don't worry about how you'll achieve it, just envision it.
- **P - Practice consistently:** Understand that progress is gradual. Improvement comes from daily learning and consistent practice.

This formula is a proven pathway to improving your mindset, which in turn enhances your happiness.

Each week, review the entries in your gratitude journal. Rate your happiness on a scale of 1 to 10 and identify the activities, thoughts, or situations that impacted your well-being. Use these insights to adjust your practices and continue improving your happiness.

NOTES

CHAPTER 4: POSITIVE RELATIONSHIPS

"Investing in our social relationships can be a powerful path toward a happier and longer life."

The Importance of Positive Relationships and Their Impact on Happiness and Longevity: Example of the Blue Zones

The "blue zones" are regions in the world where people live significantly longer and enjoy a better quality of life. These areas include Okinawa in Japan, Sardinia in Italy, Nicoya in Costa Rica, Ikaria in Greece, and Loma Linda in California. A common factor in these communities is the strong network of social relationships, which plays a crucial role in happiness and longevity.

Focus on Social Relationships

In the blue zones, social relationships are considered a priority. People maintain close connections with family, friends, and neighbors, fostering a profound sense of community and support. Here are some key aspects:

- **Mutual Support**: Strong social relationships provide emotional and practical support. This can include assistance in times of need, which reduces stress and improves mental health.

- **Community Participation**: Regular community activities promote ongoing connection with others. Participating in social events and traditions strengthens the sense of belonging and purpose.

- **Daily Interactions**: Daily interactions, such as sharing meals or chatting with neighbors, create an environment of continuous happiness and well-being. These connections help reduce feelings of loneliness and isolation.

Impact on Happiness and Longevity

Research shows that positive social relationships significantly impact happiness and longevity. Here are some benefits observed in the blue zones:

- **Stress Reduction**: Strong relationships help decrease stress levels by providing a support system to rely on during tough times.

- **Active Lifestyle**: Participation in community activities promotes an active lifestyle, essential for physical and mental health.

- **Sense of Purpose**: Frequent and meaningful social interactions give people a sense of purpose and connection, contributing to greater life satisfaction.

- **Better Mental Health**: People with strong social relationships are less likely to suffer from depression and anxiety, leading to a fuller and happier life.

Personal Example

A personal experience I want to share highlights the importance of cultivating positive relationships. When my father was diagnosed with cancer, he was hospitalized for the last two months of his life. This situation complicated my life as we are two siblings, and my brother lives in Miami. My mother didn't drive, so she depended on me. Due to health conditions, neither my mother nor my wife could spend the entire day at the hospital, especially considering the prolonged period we faced.

However, cultivating good relationships allowed us to overcome this difficult situation. The church my parents attended, as well as my brother and I during our youth, teamed up to transport my mother to the hospital for short visits. My son, who had experienced an accident, saw the situation and, with great effort, found a way to mount his wheelchair while supporting himself on one leg. He would arrive at the hospital to spend the day with his grandfather and best friend. Other family members also joined in. Thanks to them, the journey became more bearable.

Another story I remember was years earlier during my professional career. I had cultivated good relationships, and on one occasion, my parents' house had electrical problems after a hurricane. Electricians were unavailable due to many emergencies. I remembered someone I had met while working at the bank, and without hesitation, he asked me, "Give me the address where your parents live." He brought his employees during work hours to resolve the problem and refused to charge me anything.

Having people close in times of crisis brings peace and maintains contentment. This experience reaffirms the power of social relationships in our lives, not only during moments of joy but also, and especially, during difficult times.

I could write an entire book about the positive impact of having built a network of good relationships. All have been an enormous blessing for my family and me.

In Summary

The blue zones teach us that investing in our social relationships can be a powerful path toward a happier and longer life. Cultivating human connection not only enriches our lives emotionally but also has profound benefits for our health and longevity.

The Science of Healthy Relationships

John Cacioppo's research on loneliness shows that social connections not only improve our emotional health but also our physical health. People with strong social networks have a lower risk of heart disease and a better response to stress.

Moreover, Bowlby's attachment theory suggests that our earliest relationships (especially with primary caregivers) influence our ability to form healthy relationships in adulthood. Understanding and healing these early relationships can be a crucial step in strengthening our current connections.

Exercise to Strengthen Social Relationships

Objective:

Foster and strengthen your social relationships to improve your happiness and well-being.

Instructions:

- **List of Important People**:

Make a list of at least five people you consider important in your life. They can be friends, family, or colleagues.

- **Regular Contact**:

Commit to contacting at least one of these people every week. This can be through a phone call, text message, email, or an in-person visit.

- **Sharing and Listening**:

During these exchanges, dedicate time to share your thoughts and feelings as well as actively listen to what the other person has to say. Active listening involves paying attention, asking questions, and avoiding interruptions.

- **Joint Activities**:

Plan to do an activity together at least once a month with these people. This could be something as simple as having coffee, taking a walk, or engaging in a hobby you both enjoy.

- **Gratitude and Recognition**:

Take a moment to express gratitude and acknowledge the other person's positive qualities or actions. A simple "thank you" or a sincere compliment can greatly strengthen a relationship.

- **Details That Strengthen**:

Note in your calendar the day of their birthday, anniversary, or another important detail about them, and congratulate them. Receiving a call or message like this highlights your appreciation and strengthens the relationship, whether it's familial, professional, or friendly.

- **Personal Reflection**:

At the end of each month, reflect on how you've felt while strengthening these connections. Write down any positive changes in your well-being or happiness and set new goals for the next month.

Conclusion:

Fostering and maintaining strong social relationships requires effort and dedication, but the benefits in terms of happiness and health are invaluable. This exercise will help you establish and nurture those vital connections.

NOTES

CHAPTER 5: THE IMPORTANCE OF SELF-CARE IN HAPPINESS

"Taking time to care for yourself is not a luxury; it is a necessity."

Introduction

Had I allowed myself to be influenced by self-proclaimed doctors, trainers, counselors, and other hallway voices, I'm not sure where or how I'd find myself today. Thanks to that inner voice that kept urging me not to listen and to keep searching for the right map to deal with aging and premature health conditions that concerned me, I avoided aging prematurely. The Bible says: "For everyone who asks receives; the one who seeks finds; and to the one who knocks, the door will be opened." —Matthew 7:8.

I did exactly that—I kept praying, knocking on doors, and searching until I found it. There is a myth about exercise: many believe it means leaving the gym in pain, but you should know that it doesn't have to be that way to achieve positive results. I think this misconception is why some people reject the process of exercising. However, the truth is that the body is designed to move, not to sit still. Think about it for a moment: before cars and instant transportation existed, legs were the most common means of getting around.

When I give talks, particularly in churches, someone often cites 1 Timothy 4:8, which says, "For physical training is of some value." This is easy to explain—they didn't need additional exercise because their bodies were already in motion from walking, planting, or hunting. In other words, they were continuously active. Exercise became necessary to maintain care in light of the sedentary lifestyle that is leading many to shorten their lifespans.

Today, more and more people use electronic transport or scooters to get around. This is both sad and unfortunate because, while I recognize that these tools are a blessing for those who truly need them, they have contributed to greater inactivity for others.

Self-care is an essential part of maintaining happiness and overall well-being. In this chapter, we will explore how self-care can positively impact your life, and I will provide practical, simple strategies you can incorporate into your daily routine.

Self-Care Strategies

Physical Health

- **Example**: Marta, a working mother, began prioritizing her physical health by dedicating time to regular exercise and maintaining a balanced diet. This not only improved her health but also boosted her mood and energy levels.

- **Statistic**: According to the American Heart Association, 150 minutes of moderate exercise per week can reduce the risk of depression by 26%.

Mental Health

Engage in activities that nurture your mind, such as reading, meditating, or learning new skills.

- **Example**: Roberto found relief and satisfaction by learning photography, which helped him reduce stress and improve his mental well-being.

Positive Relationships

- **Statistic**: A Harvard University study found that positive relationships are one of the strongest predictors of long-term happiness.

Time for Yourself

Dedicate time to activities you enjoy and that allow you to recharge.

- **Example**: Carla set aside 30 minutes a day to practice painting, providing her with a creative outlet and a chance to relax.

Adequate Rest

- **Statistic**: The National Sleep Foundation recommends 7–9 hours of sleep per night for adults. Lack of sleep can negatively impact mood and physical health.

Inspiration

Laura's story, where she transformed her life through intentional self-care, is a powerful reminder that taking care of yourself allows you to be your best version for yourself and others.

Margie, one of my clients, once came to me and said: "Listen, son, I'm 50 years old, I just retired, and I've never exercised. Let's see what you can do for me." I took it as a challenge, and so did she. She transformed her life, and I couldn't be prouder of her.

I could list countless real testimonies of clients who overcame age, physical, and/or knowledge limitations, transforming their worn-out bodies into ones full of vitality and health—myself included.

Conclusion

Self-care is not a luxury; it's a necessity. By incorporating self-care practices into your daily life, you can significantly improve your productivity at work and in your personal life, extend your lifespan, and achieve things many believe are only possible in youth.

Here's a checklist of important yet simple daily practices. Before making changes to your exercise routine or diet, consult your doctor or health professional:

1. **Maintain a Balanced Diet**

   Include a variety of foods like fruits, vegetables, lean proteins, and whole grains. Avoid excessive sugar and saturated fats.

2. **Stay Hydrated**

   A common guideline is to drink half your body weight in ounces of water daily. For instance, if you weigh 150 pounds, aim for 75 ounces of water. Increase your intake if you're sweating from exercise or outdoor activities.

3. **Exercise Regularly**

   Aim for at least 30 minutes of moderate exercise 5 times a week. This can include walking, running, swimming, or any activity you enjoy.

4. **Get Enough Sleep**

   Sleep 7–9 hours per night. Proper rest is crucial for recovery and overall well-being.

5. **Avoid Tobacco and Moderate Alcohol Consumption**

   Not smoking and drinking in moderation are key to long-term health.

6. **Manage Stress**

   Practice relaxation techniques like meditation, yoga, or activities that help you unwind. Chronic stress can negatively impact your health.

7. **Have Regular Medical Checkups**

   Schedule periodic doctor visits for general checkups and preventive screenings to detect and address potential issues early.

8. **Maintain Good Hygiene**

   Wash your hands frequently, maintain oral health by brushing and flossing daily, and follow proper personal hygiene practices.

9. **Incorporate Resistance Training**

   Add resistance exercises like weightlifting or elastic bands to your routine. These help maintain and build muscle mass, essential for strength and mobility over time.

10. **Work on Flexibility**

    Include stretching and flexibility exercises like yoga or Pilates. This improves mobility, reduces injury risk, and promotes good posture.

11. **Reduce Processed Foods and Fast Food**

    Limit or eliminate highly processed foods and fast-food restaurant meals. Choose fresh, whole foods whenever possible.

NOTES

CHAPTER 6: CREATING A PERSONALIZED ACTION PLAN

"Success is not the key to happiness. Happiness is the key to success. If you love what you do, you will be successful." — Albert Schweitzer

In this final chapter of the first part, we'll consolidate everything we've learned in the previous chapters to create a personalized action plan that helps you achieve happiness and begin your personal reinvention. An effective action plan is specific, measurable, and adaptable.

Steps to Create Your Personalized Action Plan

1. Define Clear Goals

Clearly outline your goals in different areas of your life.

- **Example**: Laura set specific goals to improve her emotional and physical well-being, such as practicing yoga three times a week and meditating daily.

2. Establish Daily and Weekly Actions

Create a schedule with daily and weekly actions that support your goals.

- **Example**: Juan decided to spend 10 minutes a day writing in his gratitude journal and 30 minutes a week attending therapy sessions.

3. Track and Evaluate Progress

Keep a record of your achievements and adjust your plan as necessary.

- **Statistic**: A study from the University of Toronto found that people who track their habits in a journal are 30% more likely to reach their goals.

4. Maintain Flexibility

Be adaptable and open to changes in your interests and circumstances.

- **Inspiration**: Ana's story shows the importance of being flexible. She adjusted her action plan when she discovered new passions and areas of interest.

5. Seek Support and Accountability

Surround yourself with people who support and motivate you to reach your goals.

- **Example**: Francisco joined an online support group that helped him stay motivated and accountable for his wellness practices.

Don't forget to follow me on social media at Facebook: facebook/frankiecotto or Instagram: @frankiecotto, or join the Facebook group "Tu Bienestar es Prioridad", created for people like you who urgently and seriously want to make a change.

Conclusion

By creating and following a personalized action plan, you can maintain the focus and motivation needed to transform your life. Remember, this plan is a flexible tool that should adapt to your changing needs and circumstances.

However, it's important to acknowledge that making changes in life is often uncomfortable at first. Giving up or limit TV time, going to bed and/or waking up 15 minutes earlier to work on these changes can feel inconvenient. But once you turn these adjustments into habits, you'll find it much easier to expand those 15 minutes, and your life will transform into one filled with happiness and a sense of contribution.

NOTES

CHAPTER 7: CONTRIBUTING AND FINDING PURPOSE

"The two most important days in your life are the day you are born and the day you discover why."

Mark Twain

In the quest to find our life's purpose, each individual faces a unique and challenging journey. As Mark Twain so eloquently said, discovering our purpose is one of life's greatest revelations. This understanding begins with introspection and the courage to pursue our dreams, as illustrated in the story of Juana shared below.

Juana's Story

Juana's journey is an inspiring example of self-discovery. From a young age, she dreamed of becoming a nurse, driven by a deep desire to help others—reflecting the call to serve, as mentioned in 1 Peter 4:10: *"Each of you should use whatever gift you have received to serve others, as faithful stewards of God's grace in its various forms."*

Yet, Juana's aspirations also included a longing for a life of luxury. As she advanced in her career, she faced the common challenge of aligning her profession with her personal goals. Her story highlights that understanding one's purpose is not solely about choosing a profession. It is about integrating values, passions, and personal fulfillment into a balanced and meaningful life, as advised in Proverbs 16:3: *"Commit to the Lord whatever you do, and he will establish your plans."*

Emotional Connection and Purpose

Juana's story encourages reflection on how emotions, guided by divine wisdom, shape our decisions and help us construct our purpose. As noted in the book *Mind Hacking Happiness*, managing our emotions is essential to achieving success and happiness.

In **Philippians 4:6-7**, we are reminded of the power of inner peace: *"Do not be anxious about anything, but in every situation, by prayer and petition, with thanksgiving, present your requests to God. And the peace of God, which transcends all understanding, will guard your hearts and your minds in Christ Jesus."*

By embracing these teachings, we can forge a deeper connection with our essence and continually reinvent ourselves to lead a fulfilling and meaningful life.

Transition to Reinvention

Nelson Mandela serves as a powerful example of personal reinvention and transformative leadership. Born into a society riddled with racial injustice, Mandela dedicated himself to fighting apartheid in South Africa. His resistance led to imprisonment, where he spent 27 years in confinement. Yet, Mandela did not succumb to bitterness. Instead, he used his time to reflect, learn, and prepare for a life of service and reconciliation.

Upon his release in 1990, Mandela emerged as a global symbol of peace and unity. His transformation from a combative activist to a collaborative leader enabled him to dismantle apartheid through dialogue and reconciliation. In 1994, he became South Africa's first Black president, championing equality, social reform, and human rights.

Mandela's story embodies the essence of reinvention: turning personal suffering into a source of strength to benefit others. His legacy reminds us that even in the most adverse circumstances, we possess the capacity to grow, lead, and create positive change.

Through self-awareness, personal reflection, and emotional understanding, Mandela overcame immense challenges and transformed his experiences into a platform for empowering millions. His life serves as an enduring example of how reinvention and purpose can inspire profound impact.

The Importance of Understanding and Managing Emotions:

This contemporary example leads us directly to another crucial aspect of the journey of reinvention: the role of emotions. Like Mandela, understanding and managing our emotions is essential for transforming ourselves and achieving our personal and professional goals. This knowledge and control not only help us face challenges but also enable us to navigate life with greater balance and purpose.

From my early steps in personal improvement, I understood that we are not prisoners of our thoughts or emotions. This concept, present in books like *Mind Hacking Happiness* and biblical teachings, taught me that the first step to changing my reality was to change my perception. Just as Romans 12:2 invites us to "be transformed by the renewing of your mind," I realized that change is both an internal and spiritual journey.

Understanding the Mind:

We live in a world full of mental challenges, and learning to change my thoughts helped me live with new expectations. I recalled the message in Philippians 4:8, where we are encouraged to focus on what is true, noble, right, and pure.

In *Mind Hacking Happiness*, Shawn Achor highlights the science behind happiness, explaining that it is a state that can be cultivated through understanding and training the mind. This book teaches that our emotions result from brain processes we can influence, allowing us to take control of our mood and reactions.

Understanding our emotions is the first step toward managing them effectively. Achor explores how our brain processes emotions and how our perceptions directly impact our emotional well-being. He proposes a simple formula: Event + Interpretation = Emotion. This formula demonstrates that while we cannot always control external events, we can manage our interpretations.

Achor emphasizes the importance of practicing gratitude and optimism to reframe our interpretations. For instance, when facing a challenge, we can reframe the situation as an opportunity for growth, which not only changes our emotions but also influences the outcome of our actions.

Understanding how our brain works regarding emotions helps us manage them better and enhances our overall well-being. By consciously applying these practices in our daily lives, we can transform our experiences, maximizing happiness and success along the way.

The Power of Emotional Control:

Emotions can be tumultuous, but the Bible teaches us the importance of self-control, as Proverbs 16:32 says, "Better a patient person than a warrior." The book *Control Your Mind and Master Your Emotions* showed me how proper emotional management helped me find inner peace, similar to the peace promised in Isaiah 26:3 for those who keep their minds focused on God. Understanding that self-control is not a restriction but a form of inner freedom gave me a new perspective on facing daily challenges.

Creating Successful Habits:

In *Millionaire Success Habits*, Dean Graziosi discusses creating positive habits, a concept that resonates with James 1:22, which urges us to be doers of the word, not just hearers. My habits became daily manifestations of my faith, where small acts of discipline and love led to significant transformations.

The Mindset Shift:

Finally, in *The Millionaire Mind* by T. Harv Eker, the importance of mindset for financial success is emphasized. Similarly, Matthew 6:33 reminds us to seek first the Kingdom of God, teaching me that an abundance mindset begins with proper priorities and an understanding of true wealth.

Conclusion:

The Bible and these studies taught me that you are not defined by your past mistakes or negative experiences but by how you choose to move forward. In 2 Corinthians 5:17, we are told that if anyone is in Christ, they are a new creation. These spiritual and practical lessons have transformed my life, and I hope that by sharing them, you will also find the tools needed to build a story of success and purpose.

Final Reflection:

Keep in mind that often we desire something that does not align with our reality. Let us look at it from the perspective of Mother Teresa of Calcutta. She lived humbly but managed millions to help others, living her passion through service.

Exercise: Find Your Purpose

- Identify Your Passions: "Passion is the genesis of genius." – Tony Robbins
- Write down three things you are passionate about.
- Reflect on the Impact: "The purpose of life is to contribute in some way to making things better." – Robert F. Kennedy
- Reflect on how these passions can benefit others.
- Create an Action Plan: "A goal without a plan is just a wish." – Antoine de Saint-Exupéry
- Define a simple plan to put into practice what you believe your purpose is.

Save your responses because, as we begin the second part of this book, you will define and design your life.

Transition to the Second Part of the Book:

Like Mother Teresa and other inspiring examples, you can find and follow your purpose. In the second part of the book, we will explore practical strategies to define your purpose, reinvent yourself, and live a life filled with meaning and satisfaction.

"Finding purpose is not just a goal; it is a continuous journey. I invite you to discover how you can serve with your unique talents and build a bright and joyful future."

NOTES

PART TWO: REINVENT YOURSELF TO SERVE

INTRODUCTION

"Your work is to discover your work, and then give your whole heart to it."

Buddha

I was heading to the San Juan port in Puerto Rico to try to get my family off the island. A few days earlier, a devastating Category 5 hurricane called Maria had passed through. It destroyed everything in its path—houses, trees, and roads—leaving the island devastated. My wife and my mother had several health conditions, which meant that being without electricity, water, and food shortages would worsen their well-being.

On the way, I saw a country in ruins: downed power lines and poles on the ground, hundreds of cars lined up to buy fuel, and at other stations, large hand-made signs that read: "No Gasoline" or "No Ice." I also noticed that, even before opening, some supermarkets already had hundreds of people in line to buy food, letting them enter in groups of 10.

The situation didn't look promising for people with health conditions. My brother, who lives in Miami, was able to secure space for them on a cruise ship with a humanitarian mission. We arrived early, as I imagined that hundreds of people would also show up, trying to board the ship and make it to the United States to decide their next steps. I left them in line and went to park my car.

As I walked, I noticed a somber Old San Juan: fallen trees, dirty streets, closed businesses. Then, I heard a sharp noise coming from the sky. Looking up, I saw three military helicopters. Lowering my gaze, I saw more and more people arriving to board the cruise. Many faces reflected anguish, anxiety, and desperation to leave Puerto Rico. Some were tourists who had been stranded after the hurricane and were trying to return home. It was a scene straight out of a Hollywood movie, and I was part of it.

After several hours of shoving and arguments, my son, wife, and mother managed to board the ship. From a distance, I watched them leave, having no idea when I would see them again or what would happen to my family. It was a very sad moment for me, especially when I returned home and found it empty. That night was confusing, just like the darkness resulting from having no electricity—tenebrous as well.

What will I do? Should I have gone with them? But if I leave, it's like running away instead of facing and rebuilding the country. But how long will this reconstruction take? If none of my clients call me for work, what will I live on? These and many other questions crossed my mind, including… will I have to reinvent myself again? It's astonishing how your life can change from one day to the next without warning and without asking permission.

At that moment, I had to face the harsh reality that months of uncertainty awaited me, during which I would have to make decisions without letting my emotions control me. In other words, I needed to be objective and honest with myself about what was best for me, particularly for my family. I couldn't worry about what others might say or judge me for.

In life, I learned that many times, we make decisions to please others or don't make them because of what others might say. I firmly believe that we are all called to do something for others, but not all of us are called to save the world. People must pursue their life's mission; otherwise, years will pass, and we will not have fulfilled our purpose.

The subsequent nights turned into moments of meditation, prayer, and reflection on the steps I needed to take. I didn't understand why life was confronting me with another major giant. However, I had become a warrior who didn't accept defeat, much less saw it as something impossible to overcome.

As I mentioned in the introduction, life forced me to reinvent myself again. However, on this occasion, I learned that if I couldn't be happy without what I wanted, I would never be happy.

I discovered that I had to learn to value and be content with what I already had.

This is why I've come to understand that happiness is a fundamental pillar in our lives, and in the first part of this book, we explore its various facets and how to cultivate it. Now, in the second part, we embark on a journey of personal reinvention. This is a dynamic process that goes beyond the pursuit of happiness and leads us to rediscover ourselves, redefine our purpose, and transform our lives.

The time has come to look ahead and think about how you can transform yourself to live a life with greater purpose and satisfaction. Here's the key: This reinvention must focus on serving others. By serving selflessly, money and success will naturally follow as a result of that commitment.

As I mentioned earlier, in the first part, I shared how I experienced a real transformation when I started with my body and then my professional career. However, that wasn't the first time I lost my job or experienced personal transformation or reinvention. Without realizing it at the time, that was my final exam. In Chapter 10, I'll provide the complete course so you can take advantage of it and begin to see your life experiences—especially those you consider difficult or painful—differently.

It is this spirit of reinvention focused on service that I want to explore with you in the second part of this book. Your mission, should you choose to accept it, is to start seeing life from a new perspective, recognize your strengths and weaknesses, and discover how you can reinvent yourself to serve. We will use the foundations of happiness you've already learned and apply them to design a life that not only brings you personal satisfaction but also inspires and helps others. The money will come in due time and abundantly.

Transition To The Second Part

"Reinvention is not abandoning who you are but embracing who you are destined to be."

From Happiness to Reinvention

Reinvention doesn't mean starting from scratch or changing everything at once; it's more of an act of constant evolution. We leverage who we already are, our experiences, and our learnings to build an improved version of ourselves. Every step toward reinvention is an opportunity to align ourselves more with our true desires and potential.

As we advance on this reinvention journey, it is essential to understand that true change comes with purpose and authenticity. In this second part, we will explain practical methods and profound strategies to help you find your true passion, define your purpose, and plan every step toward the life you deserve. Get ready to discover valuable tools and reflective exercises that will accompany you at every stage of this exciting path of personal reinvention.

How Did I Come to These Conclusions and Strategies?

When I worked in banks, some of my responsibilities included conducting investigations and preparing business continuity plans. That is, I had to have an alternate plan so that, in the event of a disaster, the bank could maintain its critical processes until the worst of the emergency had passed. Afterward, the steps had to be ready to restore operations.

While facing all the difficulties I encountered, I began to integrate research concepts and adapt them to my personal life to maintain my progress. I did the same to create alternate plans for my family to overcome adversity. Most importantly, I discovered the importance of maintaining a good attitude, smiling at life, and proactively moving forward.

In this book, I want to help you gain clarity, stay focused even in challenging moments, and address other aspects of vital importance that you'll discover in the coming pages. And not only that, later, I'll show you how to monetize your passion so that you can share your purpose with others and live a life full of fulfillment.

CHAPTER 8: ACCEPTANCE AND RECOGNITION

"Recognizing and accepting our past decisions is the first step toward a full and authentic life."

I clearly remember the moment when the doctor returned to the room accompanied by two nurses. The atmosphere shifted, and I knew something was wrong. When he uttered the word "cancer," my wife, who was by my side, broke into tears. Yet, at that instant, I experienced an inexplicable inner peace, as if a part of me had already accepted that everything would be okay and that this was another necessary event for a new opportunity for spiritual growth.

Nevertheless, I asked the doctor: Why my chest if it's an area that's always covered? He asked if I had been exposed to the sun during my youth. I recalled those endless days outdoors at the beach, playing basketball in the street or at the park, under the sun, without a shirt or sunscreen. The answer was clear: yes, almost every day.

At that moment, I had to accept the reality and recognize the past decisions that led me to this point. It was a process of accepting my vulnerability and recognizing the fragility of life. Despite the uncertainty, I found solace in understanding that acceptance is the first step toward healing.

Life presents us with unexpected moments that challenge us to accept and recognize our reality. It was very interesting to experience this and see how a routine visit to the dermatologist for some spots on my legs turned into a much more significant discovery. Although the prescribed cream removed the spots, a more thorough skin check revealed something I never anticipated: cancer. However, it was even more astonishing to wonder what would have happened if the spots hadn't appeared... it might have been too late and the situation more complicated.

This journey taught me that accepting and recognizing our circumstances is essential for moving forward. It allows us to face challenges with faith, courage, and find peace, even in the midst of the storm.

To begin the path toward personal reinvention, it is essential to start with acceptance and recognition. Sometimes, people struggle with happiness because they don't fully understand the purpose of their lives. Accepting and recognizing our past decisions and circumstances allows us to let go of what does not benefit us and make space for new opportunities.

You must accept that you are where you are because of decisions you made in the past. Whether they were good or not so good, they have brought you to where you are, whether you like it or not. Forgive me for being blunt, but that's the reality, and believe me, it's not your fault. By doing this exercise, I want you to discover for yourself the reasons behind it—not to blame anyone or seek revenge, but to know whom to forgive. That will set you free.

To illustrate this concept, I want to share Marta's story. Marta had always dreamed of becoming an artist, but due to family expectations and societal pressure, she decided to study law and become a lawyer. Over the years, Marta felt increasingly dissatisfied and disconnected from her authentic self. It was only when she began to accept her true desires and recognize that she had made decisions based on others' expectations that she was able to start her journey toward reinvention.

Today, Marta has left her legal career and dedicates herself full-time to her passion for art, feeling happier and more fulfilled than ever. On her journey toward acceptance, Marta discovered gratitude for every step she took to rediscover her true passion.

Childhood Influences

From the moment of our birth until about the age of seven, we absorb a significant amount of beliefs and influences from our environment. These early experiences often shape our perceptions and decisions throughout life. Romans 12:2 reminds us:

"Do not conform to this world, but be transformed by the renewal of your mind."

It is essential to recognize these influences in order to accept them and, if necessary, reprogram our minds to align our actions with our authentic purpose.

Scientific Perspective

Neuroplasticity is the brain's ability to reorganize itself throughout life by forming new neural connections. This phenomenon shows that we are not destined to live according to the beliefs and patterns of our past. With conscious effort and practice, we can change our thoughts, behaviors, and ultimately, our lives.

Reflection Exercise: The Tunnel of Time

I invite you to do the exercise called "The Tunnel of Time." Find a quiet and comfortable place where you can relax without distractions. Close your eyes and visualize a tunnel that represents your life from childhood to the present. As you move through the tunnel, allow memories, emotions, and past decisions to emerge in your consciousness.

Steps for the Exercise:

- **Visualization:** Imagine the tunnel filled with key moments of your life, from your earliest memories to the present.
- **Reflection:** As you move through the tunnel, take note of the decisions and experiences that have had the greatest influence on your life.
- **Recognition:** Acknowledge, without judgment, the decisions you made based on others' expectations or limiting beliefs.
- **Acceptance:** Accept these decisions and experiences as part of your story, understanding that they shaped who you are today.
- **Release:** Allow those past decisions to remain behind in the tunnel as you move forward, focusing on a future filled with possibilities aligned with your authentic desires.

This exercise can be repeated whenever you need it, especially when you feel you are straying from your true desires.

Closing the Chapter

Accepting and recognizing our past decisions is the first fundamental step toward reinvention. By understanding our early influences and how they have shaped our lives, we can free ourselves from limiting patterns and open up to a more authentic and fulfilling life. I encourage you to commit to this process, carrying with you a positive affirmation that reminds you of the power of forgiveness and acceptance.

NOTES

CHAPTER 9: THE POWER OF THE PRESENT

"Happiness is enjoying the present moment without anxious dependence on memory or desire"

Thich Nhat Hanh

On one occasion, I was preparing to travel to an unknown place in search of someone who had committed fraud at the bank where I worked. I told my wife it would be a matter of two days since we had hired people who had already located the individual. We arrived at the airport and said goodbye as usual, with a kiss and a hug, not knowing what awaited me.

The trip extended, and after a week of searching, we discovered that the person had no money left: they had already spent or hidden everything obtained fraudulently. The initial agreement with the investigators was that they would receive a percentage of the recovered money. Since nothing was recovered, no one would get paid. However, to my surprise, they took me to what they called their operations center and demanded what they considered their reward for the work done.

I was alone, without a car, in a foreign country, with people I barely knew who had been recommended by a third party. At the time, cell phone signals weren't as ubiquitous as they are now. The tension increased along with my internal dialogue filled with questions and answers: *How do I get out of here? Will I ever see my family again? Who can help me?*

I went out to the yard of that desolate house, in the middle of the wilderness. I took out my phone and said a prayer asking for the miracle of a signal. When I heard my boss's voice, I felt a kind of heavenly relief. I explained the situation and the sum of money they were demanding. He reassured me and asked for the details to make arrangements. I also asked him to get me on the first flight back to Puerto Rico. The hours it took for the transfer felt eternal. Finally, they received the money and took me back to the hotel where I was staying.

I immediately called to check the details of my return flight, but more problems arose: they couldn't find any flight from the city I was in. They were searching for other airports with available flights. In my wait, desperate, I began another dialogue with myself, asking the same question: *How did I get here?*

Reflecting on that situation now, I didn't just think about the physical place I was in but also the path that had led me to experience a life event that seemed straight out of a movie. If you recall, my original desire when I was in high school was to join the military and later become a federal agent. This story should amaze you as much as it amazes me.

Life often finds a way to show you the path to experiences you desire but that aren't necessarily your life's purpose. I realized that following the advice and expectations of others, without considering my own desires and aspirations, had led me to live many experiences that didn't align with my true purpose.

You may also notice how others try to control you. Everyone wants to shape your life, tell you what to do and how to do it; leaving you unhappy with the outcomes of things they couldn't achieve themselves. They don't consider the essentials: personal fulfillment and happiness. It's curious—although I didn't join the military or become a federal agent, life led me to similar experiences.

This wasn't the first time I conducted investigations or traveled to other countries in search of criminals, but it was the first time my life was at great risk as a consequence of my profession. All I wanted was to return home and to my family. When I finally managed to return, my wife greeted me at the airport with her usual smile and hug, validating her trust and affection—crucial aspects of happiness.

The reason I share this real story, albeit with changes to protect identities, is that to reinvent yourself and be happy, you must know what you want. Accept that you are where you are because of decisions influenced by others and life experiences. It's your choice to deviate or stay on course. To change, you need an open mind willing to modify habits. The key lies in your willingness and attitude, regardless of time, age, or circumstances.

This experience taught me that one reason I wasn't where I wanted to be was the influence of others. For a time, I accepted everyone's opinions, losing my identity while trying to please everyone. Even though I achieved my professional dreams and had an enviable life, I felt something was missing. I wanted more—authentic fulfillment.

Exercise: "Moments of Presence"

Objective: Cultivate the ability to enjoy and appreciate the present moment.

Instructions:

- **Find a Quiet Place**: Look for a space where you can sit comfortably without interruptions.

- **Breathe Deeply**: Take five deep breaths, inhaling through your nose and exhaling through your mouth, focusing on your breathing.

- **Observe Your Surroundings**: Take a few minutes to use all your senses. Notice the sounds, colors, smells, and textures around you. Don't judge—just observe.

- **Write Your Observations**: In a notebook, describe what you noticed. What details caught your attention? How does it feel to be completely present?

- **Reflect**: Answer the following questions:
    - How does it feel to be fully present in the moment?
    - What obstacles usually prevent you from enjoying the present?
    - What can you do daily to incorporate more moments of presence into your life?

NOTES

CHAPTER 10: CLARIFY

"What is essential is invisible to the eyes."
Antoine de Saint-Exupéry

On the path of personal reinvention, clarity is one of the fundamental pillars. We live in a world full of opinions, advice, and voices that, while often well-intentioned, can divert us from our path and cloud our vision. They tell us what we should do, what's best for us, and little by little, our decisions may become influenced or even determined by others.

The Path to Clarity

To achieve clarity, it is vital to recognize our true passions and values. Below, we'll explore how we can unmask those external voices and fine-tune our internal compass to make decisions aligned with our true selves.

Clarity not only means knowing what you want but also understanding why you want it. Being clear on this will help you make decisions based on your core values, not on the expectations imposed by others.

Clarity in a World of Distractions

In a world with so many options and countless distractions—technology, overwhelming information—it can be quite difficult to find clarity.

However, most people don't understand the importance of having this clarity and the significant role it plays. For instance, if you're not clear that your time is worth more than $10 an hour (just as an example), you'll continue working for that amount. Clarity forms the foundation for conviction, commitment, capability, consistency, and confidence.

The most important things you must protect at all times are your confidence and focus. Simply put, when you lose them, it's very difficult to regain them. And I'm not talking about confidence in others but the confidence you have in yourself and what you can achieve. Focus, on the other hand, will help you keep your gaze fixed on what aligns with what you want to achieve.

I constantly reflect and ask myself if my actions reflect the quality of the person I want to be and can be. If the answer is no, I ask how quickly I can make adjustments to achieve congruence with my vision. Those who will accomplish extraordinary things tomorrow know that the key is in what they're doing today.

Clarity is powerful because it gives you certainty. At this initial stage, you don't need to know exactly how you'll achieve what you want, but you must have great clarity about where you want to go, what you want to have, what and with whom you want to enjoy, and who you want to become.

When I started observing the lifestyle of bank executives, I knew what I wanted to achieve. However, I had no idea how to achieve it. But I began to believe it. I had clarity even though I didn't yet have the full map.

I remember my brother-in-law, who is a lawyer, giving me several suits he no longer used, as well as ties and shoes. He also had a leather briefcase he no longer needed. I used everything with great enthusiasm and hope. However, what I carried in the briefcase was a thermos for my lunch and my dreams that one day I'd be carrying important documents. The reality was that I started walking like an executive and believing it, too. I've validated that faith is believing in what you don't yet see but have conviction will happen.

By knowing where you want to go, you can begin setting goals, objectives, vehicles, routes, actions, and other steps. When you combine focus with clarity, conviction, and commitment, excuses lose power exponentially, and your capacity to grow expands naturally.

I once heard Tony Robbins share an anecdote about learning to drive racecars. The first thing he was taught was how to react when the car lost control. He was told the car would start spinning, but he shouldn't focus on the wall—instead, he should focus on where he wanted to go. The instructor emphasized, "If you keep your eyes on the wall, you'll end up crashing into it."

Interestingly, years later, I was driving my car, and for a few seconds, my attention drifted to the right. When I looked back at the road, I saw the cars ahead of me had stopped. Everything happened very quickly, but as you've probably experienced, in a matter of seconds, you imagine countless scenarios—from crashing, to riding in an ambulance, to repair costs, and more. I remember noticing a space between the car I was about to hit and a streetlight pole on the right side. I realized my car could fit through that space, so I maneuvered in such a way that no accident occurred.

What I want you to understand is the importance of not diverting your attention from what you want to achieve. Along the way, you'll encounter many distractions, influences, and obstacles that you'll need to overcome. However, if you know what you want, why you want it, and your life's purpose, you'll achieve what you set out to do.

Personal Story

As we've seen in my case, a lack of clarity led me to make decisions based on others' expectations and opinions, leaving me feeling lost and disoriented. It's a reminder that we must take the time to truly understand who we are and what we want before making crucial decisions in our lives.

In my early days, I was very insecure, to the point where I thought I wouldn't last long at the bank because I believed I couldn't do the job well. My words became a prophecy. Has it ever happened to you that when you anticipate something negative, it happens later? What we say about ourselves, we hear, and we make it a reality. However, God had other plans. Indeed, my supervisor wanted to fire me in the second week. But when you do good, have faith in God, you're not left alone.

The other person working in the department asked the supervisor to let him train me. When he started teaching me, I again expressed my negativity and lack of confidence. He got upset, stopped, looked me in the eye, and very seriously said: "Don't ever say you can't do it again. You'll succeed, but you have to change your mindset." That was the first supportive message I had heard in a professional environment. Two months later, I was managing and mastering all the responsibilities of my position.

The first time I was left without a job was like a nightmare. The bank, where I thought I'd spend 30 years before retiring, was closed in 1984 by the Federal Deposit Insurance Company (FDIC), the agency regulating banks. It had been my first formal work experience—it was my family—and now I had to decide what to do again. My daughter was barely eight months old and had a condition that prevented her from retaining milk, her sustenance. My concern grew due to health insurance and income.

It's very interesting when you begin to understand the impact your thoughts have on everything you do. In the first year, I realized my job could be done by a machine, which happened about eight years later. But we'll discuss that later; I want to guide you so that you don't overlook details in your daily life because you might miss opportunities.

Another thing I validated was seeing opportunities where no one else does. Now, I'll tell you something very ironic but from which you can learn as much as I did. Going back to the moment when the bank closed, the FDIC announced they would recruit 30 people. I got excited and went to Human Resources to get the job application that all interested people needed to fill out. I was walking down the hall when my supervisor—the one who had taught me not to give up and to believe in myself—stopped me. Looking at the application I held in my hand, he said: "If you don't know English, don't even try."

It was a blow I didn't expect. Sometimes, the messenger who helped you at one point in life becomes your greatest obstacle. The way to interpret it is that it's not the messenger but something divine that's intervening in your favor. Therefore, keeping your eyes on divine power is key, regardless of who you've chosen to believe in. He went his way, and I went mine while talking with God. That's when I decided to face my fears and reality. I said to Him: If you're in this, and I'm selected, I know you'll help me.

Days before, another bank had contacted me to offer me a job doing something I had already identified as a job that would eventually end. What do I do? The pressure of being unemployed dominated my decision, and even though it wasn't what I wanted, I decided to accept it while waiting for a response from the FDIC. I started, and the days of waiting felt eternal.

One day, during my lunch break, I went out for a walk. I looked at the sky and started a conversation with my God. I prayed: Father, if it's Your will that I stay in this job, I will do so in obedience. However, if not, I beg You to take me out of here. I was desperate.

Life's pressures will push you, if they haven't already, to make decisions far from your desires. This is the greatest reason for professional or work-related disappointments that can confuse you and lead you down the wrong path until your peace and happiness are stolen. After that walk, where even tears fell from my eyes, I returned to the office.

Interestingly, I had a message from a former colleague at the bank. I immediately called her, and she told me she saw my name on the list of those selected and that I needed to report the next day. It was a very difficult decision because I would have to call out, and I didn't want to be absent so soon in a new job. My father had taught me to be responsible and I guess it was in my DNA. However, my shift started at 4:00 PM, and the interview would be in the morning. I showed up early to try to get a good turn for the appointment.

When I heard my name, I stood up from the chair and felt my legs trembling. I was very nervous and excited at the same time. On the one hand, I knew I was facing a challenge, unsure if I could meet the requirement of speaking English. On the other hand, I was thrilled at the possibility of working for a prestigious federal agency.

I entered the office where the director of human resources and the head of operations were located. They took my file and informed me that I had been selected. They began by telling me the title and job description. At the end, they told me the salary for the position, which, to my surprise, was double what I earned at the bank. Have you ever felt like you were losing something, only to realize later that it was the best thing that could have happened to you? From believing I had lost a good opportunity, I now had a better job with excellent benefits.

My mind took control of my thoughts to the point that I was already imagining how my wife would respond when I shared the news. As soon as they finished, they paused, looked at me, and asked, "Do you accept the terms and the job?" I wanted to answer professionally, but my nerves betrayed me, and instead, I burst into laughter. Yes, just as you read, I couldn't stop laughing to the point that they looked at each other and started laughing with me.

I apologized, thanked them, and left the office to find the nearest phone to call my wife. We both began crying and laughing at the same time. That experience taught me not to rush or despair until I had all the details of my reality.

Now, I only had to face the language barrier.

I attended my first meeting where they would explain my responsibilities, and as they had warned, everything was in English. I didn't understand anything they were saying. However, across the table sat another colleague who also worked at the bank and had been selected. Her body language suggested she understood everything, so I relaxed, thinking she would explain everything to me after the meeting.

Once the meeting ended, they left the conference room, and immediately our eyes met. I asked her about the tasks, to which she replied that she hadn't understood anything and thought I had. What?! And now, what do we do? I don't know if it was part of their plan or if they realized neither of us had understood anything. But I saw an angel walk in, and when she started speaking Spanish, I felt an immense peace and joy.

I was able to confirm within myself not to despair and that God was involved in this situation. However, I only worked in that position for two days, as they reassigned me to the investigations department due to my experience. My first task was to read the bank's Board of Directors' minutes and translate them into English. That wasn't impossible since I could use a dictionary. From that experience, I want you to learn to keep your eyes wide open to opportunities, not the impossible.

What Science Says

Studies have shown that mental clarity is directly related to personal happiness and satisfaction. Research in positive psychology suggests that having a clear vision of our goals and personal values helps us stay focused and motivated.

Exercise: Find Your North

I invite you to do the following exercise to discover and clarify your values and passions:

- Find a quiet place where you can reflect without interruptions.

- Make a list of all the activities you are passionate about and make you feel alive.

- Ask yourself why each of these activities is important to you. What fundamental value do they represent?

- Reflect on whether you are living aligned with those values in your daily life.
- Write a personal mission statement that incorporates your passions and values.

This exercise, called "Find Your North," will help you clear the external noise and focus on what truly matters to move forward with coherence toward your reinvention.

Final Thought of the Chapter

"Clarity is not a destination but a continuous journey of self-exploration and alignment with our authentic selves."

NOTES

CHAPTER 11: STARTING POINT

"Self-knowledge is the first step toward reinvention."
Unknown Author

One of the first steps in your journey of reinvention is self-analysis. To move forward, you need to know where you stand, especially in fundamental areas that impact our happiness and ability to renew ourselves.

Start by defining how you feel regarding your health, finances, and relationships, as well as the state of your mind, body, and spirit. Ask yourself if you are progressing and if you feel the freedom of having chosen the path to follow. You may wonder, what do these topics have to do with reinvention? I probably would have thought the same as you, a few years ago.

However, when I went through the experience of losing everything, I was able to reassess their importance, and in fact, it became the topic of my second book, titled *"Your Well-being Is a Priority."* Reinvention is not about running after money—because, you know what? Money is always faster. Material things won't make you happy; I learned to be content when I had everything, but also when I lost… EVERYTHING.

However I don't want you to get confused. I believe we should seek prosperity and have resources to bless others. Money in good hands is powerful, and when you have clear priorities on how to use it, it is a great blessing. Now, when you are clear on your priorities and align the foundations you will learn, you will be prepared to enjoy your life to the fullest.

Think about it for a moment—without an orderly mind, meaning if you are depressed or have low self-esteem, there is no way you can focus on achieving your life goals. Now, let's say your mind is clear, but if your body lacks energy, is overweight, or unhealthy, you won't be able to live at your best either.

When I lost everything, I was able to face adversity because I had a clear mind and a healthy body. But what sustained me the most was having a strong spiritual life. During adversity, there wasn't much I could do; only my faith in God kept me at peace. Difficult moments are a sign that we are alive—believing in God, a supreme being, the universe, or whatever you believe in will give you the hope you need to keep moving forward.

Let's say your mind, body, and spirit are healthy, but you don't feel like you're progressing. You won't feel satisfied with yourself either, simply because we are designed to grow as human beings, professionals, or entrepreneurs.

Finally, I will help you evaluate where you stand regarding your finances and relationships and their importance in combining everything with the experiences you want to have while living. All of this will give you the freedom to become the person you need to transform into to live your life's purpose. Many people feel trapped in a tormenting relationship, a job they hate, or finances that do not allow them to offer their family a better quality of life.

As I told you in the introduction, during the time I had to face adversity, incorporating these elements to define my action plan for reinvention was key. Now you understand the importance of knowing exactly the state of your mind, body, and spirit, in addition to your financial, time, and relationship freedom.

The reinvention process will be more effective, and you will achieve great results in less time if you know where you stand and which of these areas need priority attention. That does not mean you won't address what will make you your best version or bring the results you desire, but if you follow this process, you will be more effective.

To help you define your work plan, later you will find exercises that will help you identify where you stand in relation to these important areas, but we will address them individually, as I will explain in the following pages. This will give you: **"Your Starting Point."**

Before any major change, it is crucial to understand our current situation, as I have already mentioned. This exercise will guide you through a self-analysis process, evaluating five essential areas for happiness and reinvention: **mind, body, spirit, finances, and relationships.** These areas are the foundation of a balanced and fulfilling life.

Reviewing the Importance of Comprehensive Health

- **Mind**
  Our mental health plays a crucial role in how we face challenges and enjoy life. Without a healthy mind, experiencing true and sustained happiness can be a challenge.

- **Body**
  Physical well-being not only impacts our health but also how we feel emotionally and mentally. A healthy body can give us the energy needed to pursue our goals.

- **Spirit**
  Our values, beliefs, and life purpose form the foundation of our spirit. Cultivating this area gives us a sense of peace and direction.

- **Finances**
  Financial stability allows us to focus on our passions without the constant stress of meeting our basic needs. Understanding and managing our finances is fundamental to a balanced life.

- **Relationships**
  Healthy and supportive relationships are vital to our happiness. Our relationships can inspire us and give us strength during difficult times.

Personal Story

When I got married and worked in my first experience in the banking industry, I earned $550.00 a month. Every month, I would tell my wife, *"Don't worry, my love, when I earn 50 or 100 dollars more, we will be fine."* This went on for several years until I was promoted to vice president. Over time, my story changed because I had focused so much on my career that when I reached 40 years old, I realized my body was worn out, I was overweight, and my health had deteriorated. I had neglected my health.

Then, the story changed. Now it was: *"When I lose a few pounds and exercise, I will be fine."* That is why the word *"well-being"* rearranged reads *"being well,"* and that is what I want you to understand and discover for yourself. I want you to choose and be well, but on your own terms and desires.

Positive psychology and the science of happiness highlight the interconnectedness of these life areas. Research has shown that improvement in one area, such as physical health, can have a positive domino effect on other areas, such as mental health and finances.

Exercise: The Life Map

To understand your starting point, I propose the following exercise:

- Draw a large circle on a sheet of paper and divide it into five equal sections. Each section will represent one of the areas mentioned: mind, body, spirit, finances, and relationships.

- Evaluate each area from 1 to 10 based on your current level of satisfaction, where 1 is very dissatisfied and 10 is completely satisfied.

- Color each section according to the score you gave yourself. The idea is to visualize which areas need more attention.
- Reflect on the following questions:
    - Which areas are most balanced?
    - Where do you feel the most dissatisfaction?
    - What steps could you take to improve the areas with the lowest scores?
- Write a specific action plan for each area. For example, if your physical health needs attention, you could set the goal of exercising three times a week, hiring a trainer, or finding someone with similar interests to support each other.

Action Plan:

- **Mind:**
    - Goal: [Set your goal here]
    - Actions: [List specific steps]
- **Body:**
    - Goal: [Set your goal here]
    - Actions: [List specific steps]
- **Spirit:**
    - Goal: [Set your goal here]
    - Actions: [List specific steps]

- **Finances:**
    - Goal: [Set your goal here]
    - Actions: [List specific steps]
- **Relationships:**
    - Goal: [Set your goal here]
    - Actions: [List specific steps]

This exercise, called *"The Life Map,"* will give you a clear vision of your current situation and help you identify the areas that need more focus and work. The circle doesn't have to be perfect, but if for you is too complicated, just compare your lower score all the way up until your highest result. This way it will be easy for you to identify your priorities.

NOTES

CHAPTER 12: WHAT DO YOU WANT TO BE, HAVE, AND ENJOY?

"Defining your desires is the beginning of the path to a full and authentic life."

Introduction

I love this part—it's like when you used to ask for Christmas or birthday gifts, or any other wish. Do you remember? You could barely sleep, your heart raced as the day approached. The big difference now is that this is real, it's possible, and I want you to enjoy the design process. I'm here to help you, but remember that this is about your life and your future. It's not about me—it's about you—so put in the effort.

As a child, I would listen to adults talk about their lives, their frustrations, what the new generation should or shouldn't do, what they would have done differently, or what they would never do again. If you lived the same experience, then you started believing what was possible and what wasn't. You created your reality, whether it was true or not. This is one of the reasons why many people don't live their dreams or the life they deserve.

I remember hearing them refer to people who lived near us in a higher-value area, or those they defined as the "rich folks," the "whites," or the ones from the "fancy side," often in a derogatory way. There was a time when I didn't want to have money because I associated it negatively, until I started growing up and realizing how wrong I was.

At the first bank where I worked, one of the executives invited us to a party at his house. When I arrived, we were warmly welcomed, and I saw that having money didn't make everyone arrogant. Then, I observed the comfort in which his children lived and how beautiful his house was. I was only 23 years old, and it was then that I started wanting that kind of life—but my desire was to be able to bless my family.

Transforming my way of thinking and seeing what I wanted to be, have, and enjoy allowed me to experience extraordinary moments with my family. So get ready to think differently and build a new future for yourself and your loved ones. Don't worry about whether it's possible or how you'll achieve it—we'll work on that later. Outline what you want to accomplish.

Our Beliefs and Limitations

My humble upbringing and childhood influences created doubts in me. I wondered if it was right to desire material things and if that meant I was straying from being a good person. But then I understood that wanting more for myself and my family wasn't a sin—it was a motivation to grow and contribute positively.

Limiting beliefs often arise from the experiences and messages we receive during childhood. If you grew up hearing that wealth is synonymous with arrogance or that only certain people can achieve success, those beliefs are likely still holding you back today. To achieve your dreams, it is essential to identify and challenge these limiting beliefs.

This mindset can influence how you respond to new opportunities and challenges. Overcoming it requires a conscious and constant shift in your mentality; adopting new ways of thinking that align with your values and goals.

Scientific Perspectives

The psychology of success suggests that having clear goals and high aspirations can be a powerful driver for personal fulfillment. According to studies in positive psychology, having a clear vision of what you want to be, have, and enjoy acts as a compass that guides your actions and decision-making.

Exercise: Your Desire Map

- **Step 1:** Take a moment to reflect on your dreams and desires. Write them down without restrictions—what do you want to be, have, and enjoy in your life?

- **Step 2:** Categorize your desires into three groups: **Be, Have, and Enjoy.** Be specific and detailed in each group.

- **Step 3:** Evaluate each of these desires. Ask yourself the "why" behind each one. What motivates your desire? How does it align with your values and life purpose?

- **Step 4:** Create a concrete action plan to get closer to each of these desires. What steps do you need to take to turn these aspirations into reality?

Remember, life is not just about dreaming—it's about having the courage to define and fight for those dreams. Clarifying what you want to be, have, and enjoy is the first step in turning your aspirations into reality. Every goal you set, no matter how small, is a promise to yourself that you deserve a full and happy life. Move forward with determination and confidence, knowing that the power of reinvention is in your hands.

Transforming your life starts with defining what you truly want to be, have, and enjoy. This is not just an exercise in superficial wishes but a deep acknowledgment of your right to aspire to a fulfilling and satisfying life. So go ahead, create your desire map, and start paving the way toward a bright future. Remember, you deserve a life filled with all the wonderful things you dream of.

NOTES

CHAPTER 13: DISCOVER YOUR SUPERPOWERS

"I am not who you think I am, I am not who I think I am, I am who I think you think I am."

Charles Horton Cooley

Introduction

I firmly believe that we all came with a life mission and unique superpowers that help us fulfill it. In his book *The Alter EGO Effect*, Todd Herman makes a fascinating analogy about who the real person is between the character of Clark Kent and Superman.

Most people say that Superman is the real one, but Todd Herman makes us see that the true person is Clark Kent. Clark is the child who arrived on planet Earth with superpowers and decided to keep them hidden until he clearly understood his mission. He used the character of Superman to fulfill his life's purpose, always aware of his weakness—kryptonite—and protecting himself from it as much as possible.

External Influences and Limiting Beliefs

As we grow, society shapes us, telling us what we should or shouldn't do—something I have repeated many times. They make us believe what our strengths are and weaken us by highlighting our imperfections.

These influences become ingrained in our subconscious, forming our adult personality. However, you can change this by focusing your awareness on eliminating limiting beliefs to live to the fullest.

Personal Reflection

I ask you, do you know what your weaknesses and strengths are? To perform well in your personal and professional life, it is essential to know them. Identify five or more strengths and the same number of weaknesses. Once you recognize them, you will know where to focus your attention. In the next exercise, you will discover your life mission and what you have to achieve it—your superpowers.

Personal Story

From a young age, I was always drawn to the idea of understanding my own abilities and limitations. Like Clark Kent, there were forces in my life that tried to define who I should be and how I should behave. But I always knew that within me, there was something more—something hidden, waiting to be discovered.

I remember an occasion while working at a bank, surrounded by successful colleagues with strong personalities. I often asked myself whether I had what it took to stand out like them. Through self-reflection and understanding my own strengths and weaknesses, I began to unlock my superpowers and use them to advance in my career and personal relationships.

Scientific Perspectives

Psychological research shows that understanding and using our strengths can significantly increase our happiness and success. According to studies in positive psychology, self-knowledge—especially in terms of strengths and weaknesses—is crucial for personal and professional fulfillment.

Exercise: Discover Your Superpowers

Step 1:

Take a quiet moment to reflect on your experiences and achievements. Write down five or more strengths you possess. Be specific and detailed.

Step 2:

Do the same for your weaknesses. Remember, identifying areas for improvement is the first step to strengthening them, which means having the help in a specific area.

Step 3:

Identify situations where your strengths have shined and how you have managed your weaknesses. What tactics have you used to minimize the impact of your weaknesses?

Step 4:

Reflect on your life mission. If you have already done the exercise to discover your life's purpose, you should have a clear idea of what your mission is. Now, analyze how your strengths—your superpowers—can help you fulfill that mission.

Step 5:

Develop an action plan. How can you use your superpowers to move forward on your path to your purpose? What concrete steps can you take to protect yourself from your "kryptonites" and enhance your strengths?

Inspirational Note

Remember, your superpowers are key pieces to achieving your dreams and fully living your life mission. Identifying your strengths and weaknesses is only the first step; the real power lies in how you apply them. You have control over your destiny, and every day is an opportunity to discover and strengthen those superpowers that will make you unstoppable.

NOTES

CHAPTER 14: VALUES AND PRINCIPLES

"Values are the stars that guide us; principles are the map that helps us navigate through life."

The importance of having a clear understanding of your values and principles during the transformation process is a complement that we cannot leave out.

Connection between Values, Principles, and Goals:

On the path to personal reinvention and the pursuit of happiness, it is crucial that our values and principles align with our goals. Values represent what we consider important and meaningful in life and can change over time as we evolve. On the other hand, principles are the immutable rules that guide our behavior. When we consciously align these elements with our goals, we create a solid framework for making decisions that bring us closer to authentic happiness.

To keep this topic as simple as possible while ensuring you understand it, I will use the following analogies. Principles are universal rules that cannot be changed, whereas values are those you learned from a young age. If you grew up believing that stealing to give to the poor is not wrong, you will steal all your life without feeling bad or guilty. However, if the police catch you, you will probably go to jail—simply because stealing is a principle, a law that cannot be changed.

Similarly, the law of gravity exists whether you believe in it or not. But for the sake of our example, let's say you decide not to believe in it. To prove your point of view, you get on a plane and jump without a parachute, claiming that you will not fall because, in your opinion, you do not believe in the law of gravity. What happens next? Exactly—it is very likely that you will die or be severely injured.

Impact of Misalignment:

If our values and principles are not aligned with what we wish to achieve, we may feel stuck or frustrated. Imagine wanting to experience a full and happy life but holding onto values that prioritize external results over internal well-being. This misalignment can prevent us from achieving the satisfaction and fulfillment we all long for.

Benefits of Alignment:

On the other hand, when our values and principles align with our goals, our actions reflect our true priorities. This alignment provides us with clarity and direction, allowing us to live in harmony with whom we are and what we truly want to achieve. In turn, this facilitates the enjoyment of a full and satisfying life.

Therefore, before pursuing any goal, dream, or life aspiration, you must consider your values and principles. If you do not do so, there may be a conflict between your goal and them. If your values and principles are not aligned with your goal or what you want to achieve, you will not obtain the result that every human being desires—happiness.

Some examples of values are honesty, respect, responsibility, tolerance, and integrity.

Examples of principles include life, love, freedom, peace, and justice.

Therefore, you must have a clear understanding of what your values are and what established principles exist that could conflict with what you want to achieve in your transformation. If you follow all the material I am teaching you, it is very likely that you will realize that some things you believed or were made to believe are not true. Those will fall under the category of values that you can change. On the other hand, you might discover that you have been going through life trying to break a principle that, if violated, could bring you serious consequences.

Now, it is important that you review the list of principles and values to identify those that, in one way or another, could affect your transformation.

Respect	Justice	Tolerance	Honesty
Love	Equity	Peace	Responsibility
Loyalty	Ambition	Sensitivity	Gratitude
Humility	Audacity	Prudence	Freedom
Kindness	Temperance	Creativity	Self-respect
Empathy	Abundance	Commitment	Perseverance
Joy	Health	Family	Aggressiveness
Solidarity	Wisdom	Self-control	Compassion
Dignity	Modesty	Courage	Kindness
Daring	Competitiveness	Adaptability	Trust

Final thought:

The alignment of our personal values and principles with our goals and actions is fundamental to achieving authentic happiness. It is not only about knowing what we value but also about living in coherence with these principles day by day. This coherence prepares us to face challenges with integrity and provides us with an internal compass that guides our decisions and actions.

Conclusion and Transition:

Just as our values and principles guide us in our daily lives, finding our purpose gives us a deeper reason for our being. As we transition into the next chapter, let us reflect on how a clear purpose can unlock a renewed sense of direction and meaning. It is the pursuit of something greater than ourselves that can ignite our passion and motivate us to live fully.

NOTES

CHAPTER 15: THE SEARCH FOR YOUR PURPOSE

"The mystery of human existence does not lie only in being alive, but in finding something to live for."
Fyodor Dostoevsky

The Search

Since childhood, I was very curious and daring. My grandparents lived in the countryside, in a neighborhood called "Dajaos." A beautiful place that my brother, cousins, and I loved. Playing on the land around my grandparents' house was a delight, but always within sight of my mother. Nearby, there was another abandoned wooden house that was almost collapsing; it was dirty, with floors covered in pigeon droppings that my mother claimed belonged to witches, with holes in the floor and a roof nearly falling apart.

To get there, we had to cross the street in front and walk through another piece of land. However, being naturally curious, we also discovered a kind of tunnel that ran underneath the road. My mother told us that there were snakes in the tunnel and that the house belonged to witches to keep us close to her. Nevertheless, I armed myself with one of my grandfather's old machetes, some sticks, and we set off on an adventure to discover the snakes and witches. I remember leading the way, followed by my cousins and brother. Although my heart was pounding, curiosity was stronger.

We crossed the tunnel and headed toward the house. Getting through without seeing any snakes made us feel victorious. But the witches were still unaccounted for, and my heart started beating even faster as we got closer to the old house. Upon arrival, we searched but found nothing—until we heard my father loudly calling for us, with my mother waiting to scold us. The adventure was over, but I felt satisfied, secretly celebrating the pride of having dared.

When you set out to discover your life's purpose and the time comes to start something new, you will feel fear and uncertainty. Others will do everything possible to confuse you even more—some out of protective love, but others out of envy that you are trying to achieve what they never dared to attempt. They will tell you all kinds of stories to discourage you from pursuing your dreams or reaching your goals.

It is important to understand that life is a long journey, which, in the end, you will realize was actually short and left things undone.

That is when regret sets in—not for failures, but for not having tried. My philosophy is to complete my life's mission feeling pleased with my efforts, empty because I gave my best for the improvement of others, and having used my talents in service to God and the world around me.

That is why I consider myself a student of life and a messenger of truth. You may wonder, *what is that truth?* My answer is simple: *"The truth will be whatever you decide to believe."* I have not always made the best decisions; I have failed at times and made many mistakes. However, I want to share my definition of life: to me, it means never stopping the pursuit of continuous improvement and fulfilling my purpose while I live. No one is perfect, but the satisfaction of feeling fulfilled is a wonderful happiness.

Let me ask you another question: If you could make one decision right now to set yourself on the path to your best destiny, what would it be? Would you save or invest more money? Would you change careers? Would you decide to travel more? What choice do you think would make you feel satisfied at the end of your days when looking back at all you have experienced?

Imagine your life projected on a movie screen, where your friends, family, and even people you never met personally—yet somehow were impacted by your life—are watching. What would you be pleased to see and hear?

When I celebrated my fiftieth birthday, my daughter surprised me with a video compilation of meaningful moments from my first fifty years of life. It was a touching reminder of all the wonderful experiences, unimaginable achievements, and the legacy I had left for those I had been able to bless. At that moment, I realized I had not truly appreciated all those experiences. Instead of staying in the past, I decided to create a list of the achievements and experiences I wanted to have over the next fifty years of my life—or however long God allows me to live. Then I asked myself: *What would I need to fully live this new stage?*

To reinvent yourself and find happiness, it is essential to recognize that the results you have achieved so far are your responsibility, as I mentioned earlier. Whether you feel satisfied with your current situation or not, you cannot blame your job, bad luck, or fate. Likewise, you cannot blame yourself either.

I ask that, even though this process may be painful, you embrace it as necessary. Do not try to justify, blame, or evade your responsibility, as that will only keep you stuck where you are now. The fact that you have opened this book to explore its content and how it can help you means you are searching for a change. It could be in your relationship, your job, finances, or simply because you feel you were created for something more meaningful.

Conclusion

We have explored the importance of finding our personal purpose and how it can guide us toward a more meaningful and fulfilling life. However, purpose does not exist in a vacuum. It is often intertwined with our passions—those activities and topics that deeply excite us and fill us with energy.

As we move on to the next chapter, I invite you to reflect on the passions that have been present in your life. How do they connect with the purpose you are discovering? Is there harmony between what you love to do and the impact you want to have on the world?

In the next chapter, we will delve into the difference between passion and purpose and how each plays a crucial role in our journey toward happiness and personal fulfillment. As we move forward, stay open to the possibility that your passions may be the compass guiding you toward a greater purpose.

Exercise to Discover Your Purpose

To discover your superpowers and your purpose, I propose an exercise. Reflect on the following:

- **Value to Others:** Consider how you can use your passions and talents to improve the lives of others.

This exercise will not only help you identify your superpowers but also align your passion with your life's purpose. However, it is important to understand that they do not always align, but when they do, you are more than fortunate. Let me explain: When I worked in banks, I loved what I did. However, my best moments—when I truly felt I was experiencing my passion—happened outside the office. It was when I served as a youth counselor, basketball coach, or trained people seeking better health.

To discover your superpowers and your purpose, I propose a simple exercise:

1. **Activities that Energize You:** Write down activities you enjoy so much that you lose track of time.
2. **Natural Talents:** Identify skills you are naturally good at—those that people around you always notice and comment on.
3. **Significant Contribution:** Think about times when you made a meaningful contribution to someone's life. What were you doing? How did others feel?
4. **Value to Others:** Reflect on how you can use your passions and talents to improve the lives of others.

This exercise will not only help you identify your superpowers but also align your passion with your life's purpose. In the next chapter, we will begin to differentiate these concepts and shape what will become your mission.

NOTES

CHAPTER 16: PURPOSE AND PASSION

"Passion will make you happy, and your purpose will serve others."

The Difference Between Passion and Purpose

It is very important not to confuse the meaning of these two profound words. Just like superhero characters, we all have a mission to fulfill while we are alive. However, true purpose goes beyond that. It is something that adds value to others and connects you to a broader mission in this world.

On the other hand, you might be working at a place you like, making good money, but you keep checking the time because you can't wait to practice a sport, read, or perhaps write a book. Sometimes, I meet clients who feel drained, confused, or disengaged. When I start working with them, we discover together that what they are missing is precisely the discovery and pursuit of their purpose.

There are many methods to discover life's purpose, which are often confused with passion. To understand the difference between the two and make the process easier for you, it is important to know that passion is for you; it is what fascinates you, what you love doing, regardless of whether you get paid for it or not. It is what makes time disappear.

However, I must warn you that if you cannot identify the difference between passion and purpose, you might get lost along the way. For example, when I opened my gym, I thought it was my purpose, but in reality, what I did was build my own "playground." I realized that although I enjoyed what I was doing, it was not necessarily aligned with a greater purpose beyond myself.

Perhaps you think that what you do is your passion. But it is also possible that you grew up with low self-esteem, and after finding a job where you received training, you eventually became an expert, which boosted your self-esteem. Now, you believe that this is your passion. However, true purpose goes beyond that. It is something that adds value to others and connects you to a broader mission in this world.

The Army Analogy

Imagine an army lined up for an important mission. Each soldier has specific skills and roles, and their effectiveness depends on each one performing the right function. Similarly, discovering your purpose in life is like finding the right role for your skills and talents. Your passion is the energy you bring to the field, but your purpose is the mission that benefits the group you belong to.

The soldier who performs the right role maximizes not only their efficiency but also the positive impact on the entire unit. In the same way, when our skills are placed in the "right position," we not only find personal fulfillment but also contribute to the collective well-being.

The Baseball Field Lesson

When I was young, playing baseball fascinated me. Once, the team I was on was preparing to compete against all the teams representing their town. In the end, that team would represent Puerto Rico in the U.S. One day, a former professional player arrived at our practice. He observed us for about 15 minutes and then stopped what we were doing. I remember that I was playing shortstop, and he sent me to play catcher; he moved the catcher to second base, and so on, until half the team had changed positions.

What I learned from this experience is that life is similar. Sometimes, we get comfortable with what we do and do it well. This happens at work, school, church, and in other areas. But we are playing in the team of life; that is, God or the higher power you believe in has equipped you with talents and abilities to play in a specific position.

That change was uncomfortable for me because I was very happy playing shortstop, just like others were with their positions. But once I adapted, we became an extraordinary and more powerful team. The question is: Are you playing in the position that truly belongs to you? If we all sought to play where we are truly meant to be, this world, the company you work for, or your business would be completely different.

Reflecting on Passion and Life Purpose

Let's review what you have learned. Passion and purpose are often confused, and while they may seem similar, they are different. Passion is personal; it is what makes you feel alive and excited. Purpose, on the other hand, is what you do to benefit others. For example, you might have a passion for playing baseball, but your purpose could be to train young players to help them discover their own potential.

I have dedicated time to these topics because I consider them extremely important. Do not rush through this exercise; take the necessary time because, in the end, you will feel peace, energy, and purpose in everything you do from now on.

Exercise 1: Discovering Your Purpose – Serving Others

Your Pain is Your Purpose:

Reflect on the difficult moments you have overcome. These experiences can reveal a deep purpose, as they have equipped you with unique empathy and wisdom. Ask yourself: *"What common threads do I see among my difficult experiences?"* Your pain can become a powerful tool to guide and support others in similar situations.

Serve Through Your Personal Story:

Sharing your story has a transformative impact. By being authentic about your struggles and successes, you connect deeply with others. Vulnerability in your narrative helps inspire those seeking guidance and hope. Reflect: *"How can I share my story in a way that inspires and helps others?"*

For Young People or Those Without Significant Painful Experiences:

- **Reflect on Your Interests and Passions:** Consider what you are passionate about and what you enjoy doing. Your current interests may indicate how you can add value to the world. Ask yourself: *"What activities make me lose track of time?"*

- **Explore Your Dreams and Aspirations:** Think about what you would like to achieve in the future. Is there a goal that excites you and benefits others in the process?

- **Consider Small Contributions:** You don't need a big problem to help. Identify small but meaningful ways to impact your community or immediate surroundings.

- **Examine Your Influences and Inspirations:** Reflect on the people or experiences that have inspired you. What have you learned from them that could guide you toward your purpose?

In the end, think about how these general reflections can integrate to reinforce your search for purpose.

Exercise 2: Finding Your Passion

Instructions:

- **Explore Your Interests:** Make a list of activities that excite you and that you enjoy in your free time. Think about what you used to enjoy doing as a child. Ask yourself: *"What activities made me lose track of time when I was a child?"*

- **Evaluate Your Activities:** For each activity, describe why it brings you joy and what aspects you enjoy the most. Reflect on how you feel when immersed in these activities. Consider: *"How do these activities improve my overall mood?"*

- **Prioritize and Discover:** From your list, identify the three activities you are most passionate about. Ask yourself: *"What concrete steps can I take this week to incorporate more of these activities into my daily life?"*

- **Create a Passion Statement:** Write a statement that summarizes one or two activities that represent your greatest passion. Consider how these passions could serve others or have a positive impact. Reflect on how this statement can be a guiding light for your decisions and actions.

NOTES

CHAPTER 17:
WHAT DO YOU HAVE?

"To achieve success, you must first know what resources you have and how to use them in the best way possible."
Unknown

I remember when I embarked on my own reinvention. I understood that the key to success lies not only in knowing what I possess but also in recognizing which personal skills and qualities I can leverage. Now, I want you to learn the importance of knowing what you have before embarking on this incredible journey of reinvention.

Let's Review What You Have Learned:

You must be willing to change—something you have already demonstrated by acquiring this book.

Clearly knowing what you want to be, have, and enjoy is fundamental, and you have already worked on that. You understand the *why* behind the change and the goal you have set for yourself. Let's continue building on this knowledge.

Take Inventory of Your Resources:

Imagine you want to change the color of your house paint. You already know you want a change, you have chosen the new color, and you understand the reasons. But before you begin, you need to answer questions like these:

- Do you know how to paint? If not, you may need to consider hiring someone or seeking help.
- Do you have the necessary equipment, such as rollers and brushes?
- Do you have the time to do it?

- Do you have the budget?
- When do you want to complete the job? Will you need support to finish it?

Similarly, evaluate what you need to be effective in your mission of reinvention:

- **Love:** If you don't love what you do, you will give up at the first challenge. Reflect on which part of the process you enjoy most and how this will motivate you to keep going, even during difficult moments.
- **Time:** Dedicate specific time daily to your transformation. Consider creating a schedule with moments allocated to working on your project.
- **Commitment:** Just like in marriage vows, commit deeply to yourself. Write your own commitment vows to this reinvention process.
- **Courage:** To face challenges, especially when you feel like you can't go on pause momentarily. Then, reflect on a moment in your life when courage was necessary and how you can apply that experience now.
- **Mentorship:** Find a mentor, coach, or consultant if you feel you need guidance or support. Research recommended resources and where to find them.
- **Budget:** Plan the necessary budget just as you would for any other major project.

I am very proud of you. If you have made it this far, it means that you are not part of the average but of the select group that is prepared to succeed. Now you can turn the page—you are almost done with the first part of your mission.

NOTES

CHAPTER 18:
CONTINGENCY PLAN

"Preparation is not an act of desperation but a continuous practice of acting with foresight."

Unknown

Introduction

You've probably heard the saying, *"Hope for the best, but prepare for the worst."* This advice has guided me throughout my life, helping me face ups and downs with a positive but prepared mindset. Life has taught me that circumstances can change quickly, and it's vital to be ready for the unexpected. As another saying goes, *"Man proposes, and God disposes."*

Personal Story

My mission here is to broaden your perspective and prepare you for the unexpected.

In 2008, I had five sources of income, but by 2010, I was left with only one. Learning from these experiences has taught me that no matter how positive you are, it's always wise to have a plan B. The coronavirus pandemic is a clear reminder of the importance of being prepared for events beyond our control.

During times of crisis—just like in a hurricane or earthquake—we must use our *"emergency parachute."* Your preparation, from building a savings foundation to planning a contingency strategy, can help you get back on the right track after an emergency.

Science and Data

Research shows that having a contingency plan improves resilience. According to a study by the OECD (Organization for Economic Co-operation and Development), businesses that implemented rapid response plans during the 2008 economic crisis remained operational and recovered more quickly. This finding highlights the importance of preparing both organizations and individuals to handle the unexpected.

Exercise: Create Your Emergency Parachute

To create your own emergency parachute:

- **Identify your resources:** Make a list of all your current and potential income sources, using tools or apps that simplify this process.

- **Emergency savings:** Allocate a portion of your income to an emergency fund, covering at least three to six months of expenses.

- **Action plan:** Develop a detailed plan to activate in case of an emergency. Consider including a downloadable template that covers key contacts, necessary resources, and specific actions.

- **Support network:** Identify people in your network who can offer emotional, professional, or financial support. Share examples of effective support networks to inspire the reader.

- **Review and adjust:** Regularly review your plan and adjust it based on changes in your environment and life.

Conclusion

Planning is your security anchor for the future. Now you can turn the page—you are almost done with your mission.

NOTES

CHAPTER 19:
SUSTAIN YOUR REINVENTION

"We are not meant to reinvent ourselves alone. In the support of others, we find the strength to flourish."

Support Network

The importance of a support network in the process of personal reinvention cannot be underestimated. Supportive relationships provide emotional backing, valuable insights, and different perspectives that can guide you along your journey.

Building and Strengthening Supportive Relationships

1. **Identify your allies:**

   Recognize the people in your life who encourage you and help you grow. These can be friends, family members, mentors, or colleagues.

2. **Open communication:**

   Maintain honest and open communication with those in your support network. Share your goals, challenges, and achievements to strengthen your connection.

3. **Invest time in your relationships:**

   Dedicate quality time to the people in your network. Engage in activities together, maintain regular contact, and show genuine interest in their lives.

4. **Offer your support:**

   Reciprocity is key in any relationship. Be a pillar of support for others and offer your help when needed. This will strengthen trust and mutual commitment.

5. **Participate in communities:**

   Join groups, communities, or professional networks related to your interests. These spaces provide opportunities to connect with people who share your goals and can offer the necessary support.

"The journey toward personal reinvention is not one we should walk alone. It is in the company of others, in the connections we build, and in mutual support that we find the strength to persevere and succeed. Just as a tree extends its roots to stay firm, we strengthen our growth by nurturing and caring for our support network."

Personal Testimony: Luis's Story

Luis was a young entrepreneur who ventured into the business world with many ideas and enthusiasm. However, he faced multiple obstacles that made him doubt himself. At that moment, he remembered the advice of his grandfather, a wise man who always emphasized the importance of surrounding oneself with positive and supportive people.

Luis decided to follow that advice and began attending local entrepreneur meetings. There, he met Marta, an experienced businesswoman who became his mentor. She provided him with valuable guidance, introduced him to key people in his industry, and, most importantly, offered him unconditional support during tough times.

Thanks to her support network, Luis not only overcame his initial challenges but also established a successful business. Luis's story highlights how building and strengthening supportive relationships can make a significant difference in the journey toward reinvention and personal success.

NOTES

CHAPTER 20: EMPOWERING YOURSELF FOR THE FUTURE OF WORK: STRATEGIES AND OPPORTUNITIES

"The future belongs to those who are prepared to reinvent themselves."

Introduction

The evolution of the labor market will bring the disappearance of certain jobs but also the emergence of new professions.

In a constantly changing job market, it is crucial to be prepared to adapt to new demands and opportunities. According to a report by the World Economic Forum, by 2030, 50% of all employees are expected to need new skills due to increasing automation and digitalization.

This chapter will guide you in understanding these trends and provide strategies for professional reinvention.

Cultivating the Irreplaceable

In a world where automation and artificial intelligence are rapidly transforming the job market, every change brings a wave of new possibilities. Although some technical tasks are being delegated to machines, what truly defines our human essence is becoming our greatest asset.

Skills such as creativity, critical thinking, and social abilities are the keys to unlocking opportunities in this new labor paradigm. These skills not only complement technical capabilities but also are expected to become exceptional with the rise of automation. As Pascal Bornet mentions in his book *Irreplaceable*, authenticity in a world of artificial intelligence is the ultimate competitive advantage.

Let's take the example of those who have successfully navigated these turbulent waters. Professionals who, armed with creative thinking and emotional intelligence, have redefined their roles in their respective industries or even created something entirely new. These are our pioneers on the path to the future.

To develop and refine these human skills, we can start by committing to continuous learning. Engaging in communities that foster creativity, participating in activities that challenge conventional thinking, or practicing mindfulness to enrich critical thinking are valuable steps in this direction.

As we walk this path, it is important to remember that the power and potential of humanity only multiply in the face of technological challenges. This is our moment to reinvent ourselves, to ride the wave of change, and to emerge stronger, more authentic, and more irreplaceable than ever.

The Evolution of the Job Market

Over the years, I have witnessed how the job market has evolved with new technologies and global trends. I recall my early days in the banking sector in Puerto Rico in the 1980s when there were 22 commercial banks. By 2008, when I closed that chapter of my life, only 6 remained. This transformation reflects a similar trend in the United States, demonstrating how industries can consolidate and innovate over time.

This experience highlights the importance of not halting our progress and always being prepared for change, seeking opportunities during technological and economic transformation.

Jobs at Risk of Disappearing

In this changing context, some jobs are at risk of becoming obsolete. Routine and procedural tasks are the most susceptible, such as certain roles in manufacturing that can be automated. However, the key is to adapt and find ways to transfer our skills to new fields.

New Job Opportunities

For every job that disappears, new ones emerge. Fields such as artificial intelligence, sustainability, and the digital economy are booming. These opportunities require skills that many of us already possess, such as problem solving, creativity, and empathy.

Strategies for Personal Reinvention

- **Identify your transferable skills**: List the skills you can apply to other fields and think about how you could further develop them.

- **Stay updated**: Enroll in courses or seminars that keep you informed about market trends.

- **Adapt your mindset**: Open your mind to new possibilities and be flexible in the face of change.

Cultivating the Irreplaceable

In the book *Irreplaceable* that I previously mentioned, the importance of focusing on skills that machines cannot replicate is emphasized. Creativity, critical thinking, and emotional intelligence are fundamental to excelling in this new era. Developing these skills not only prepares you for the future but also differentiates you in the present.

Home-Based Businesses

For those who prefer to work from home, there are numerous opportunities. You can explore home-based businesses that do not require advanced technical skills but do demand strong work ethics and creativity, such as consulting, writing, or online teaching.

Jobs at Risk of Disappearing

- Data Entry Operators
- Telemarketing Employees
- Supermarket Cashiers
- Manufacturing Line Operators
- Truck Drivers
- Travel Agents
- Bank Employees
- Receptionists
- Call Center Staff
- Traditional Machinery Maintenance Technicians

New Job Opportunities

- Cybersecurity Specialists
- Big Data Analysts
- Software and App Developers
- Artificial Intelligence Experts

- User Experience (UX) Designers
- Renewable Energy Engineers
- Digital Transformation Consultants
- Digital Health Specialists
- Online Learning Facilitators
- 3D Printing Technicians

Quotes and References

The job market predictions come from accredited sources such as the *World Economic Forum* and studies from recognized consulting firms like *McKinsey & Company* and *Gartner*.

- **World Economic Forum.** (2020). *The Future of Jobs Report 2020.* https://www.weforum.org/publications/the-future-of-jobs-report-2020/
- **McKinsey & Company.** (2021). *The Future of Work after COVID-19.* https://www.mckinsey.com/featured-insights/future-of-work/the-future-of-work-after-covid-19
- **Gartner.** (2022). *Gartner Predicts the Future of Jobs.* https://www.gartner.com/en/supply-chain

Physical Jobs for the Future

For those who prefer physical work, there are several alternatives that do not require a university degree. Here are some examples:

- Renewable Energy Maintenance Technicians
- Solar Panel Installers
- Sustainable Agriculture Specialists

- Electronic Equipment Repair Technicians
- Sports and Fitness Mentors
- Entrepreneurs in Manual Services (e.g., plumbing, carpentry)
- Clean Energy Vehicle Drivers
- Advanced Recycling Technicians
- Community Health Workers
- Public and Natural Spaces Managers

Strategies for Personal Reinvention

To adapt to these new job opportunities, it is essential to follow certain strategies:

- **Continuous Education**: Participate in relevant courses and certifications.
- **Adaptability**: Maintain an open mindset toward changes and new experiences.
- **Networking**: Build a strong network of professional contacts.
- **Soft Skills Development**: Improve skills such as communication, teamwork, and leadership.
- **Technology**: Familiarize yourself with new tools and technology platforms.
- **Start a home-based business.** Starting a home-based business in network marketing can be a great way to build wealth if you put in the time and effort. It's important to know that success won't come quickly, and it's not for those looking to get rich fast.

These suggestions are merely to give you an idea of the possibilities and constant changes to which we are exposed. However, there are multiple alternatives that are constantly emerging. Therefore, you should do your own research and update accordingly.

NOTES

CHAPTER 21:
CONCLUSION

"True happiness is cultivated with every step toward your best version."

I cannot finish without highlighting people very close to me who have achieved an extraordinary reinvention and transformation. Mr. Reinaldo Cintrón, my son-in-law, and his wife Jessenia Cotto, who continually reinvent themselves, have never ceased to surprise me. Reinaldo, in addition to being a lawyer, has not left his passion nor has Jessenia. Every day they amaze me with their accomplishments, integrity, and desire to serve others. Rei, apart from his profession in the legal field, is a singer, poet, artist, Christian leader, comedian, husband, son, in short, the list is long. Jessenia, for her part, in addition to being an excellent mother and leader; She acts, is a screenwriter and they complement each other in an extraordinary way. Today, their two children have joined and as a family they make thousands laugh. You can see their work under "Uno Y Media" on social networks. Just by seeing them in action, you can feel their passion and joy in doing what they love.

Josué Cotto, who went from adapted physical education teacher, then personal trainer to finally becoming a very talented artist. But although he is a musician, he does not dedicate himself to that but is one of the topiary experts in one of the most famous parks in the United States. If you have visited Universal Studios in Orlando, you have probably seen some of his artwork on the trees, plants and flowers with different designs. If you had asked me 30 years ago who he would become, I would never have deciphered what he does today with such passion and excellence.

And finally, Terelys Porrata, a young woman who went from being a teacher, personal trainer to a very successful entrepreneur as well as a naturopath and excellent mother. Despite her achievements, she did not stop and continues studying, almost finishing a doctorate in Systemic Family Theotherapy at the time

I finished this book. This young woman came up to me the day I launched my first book and said; I want you to be my mentor. I have seen her help hundreds of people through her naturopathy practice, see her impact on social networks where you can find her under her name, as well as see her skyrocket. I have enjoyed each of her achievements as well as feeling very proud of her.

I have mentioned them to you because as we reach the end of this transformative journey, it is important to reflect on the learning's and tools we have explored together, but also leave you inspired by what is possible. We have internalized essential concepts that lead us to a happier and more fulfilling life.

We have traveled a transformative path together, exploring the fundamental keys to discovering happiness and undertaking a process of personal reinvention. From acceptance and clarification of our desires and values, to continued action and periodic adjustments, each step is vital to building a full and meaningful life.

This book is not just a guide, but also a companion on your journey of self-discovery and growth. Remember that every challenge is an opportunity to learn and every success, no matter how small, is a reason to celebrate.

Primary Key Summary

Self-care: Prioritizing our physical, mental and emotional well-being allows us to face life with greater energy and resilience.

Gratitude: Practicing daily gratitude transforms our perspective, helping us focus on the positive and cultivate optimism.

Life Purpose: Finding and living our purpose gives us clear direction and a deep sense of meaning in our actions.

Contribute to a Greater Cause: Contributing to the community and the world connects us with others and amplifies our positive impact.

Cultivate Positive Relationships: Healthy, supportive relationships are essential to our emotional well-being and happiness.

Continuous Renewal: Happiness is a dynamic process that requires constant adjustments and renewals to keep us aligned with our goals and values.

Invitation to move forward without giving up

Now that you have a series of practical strategies and exercises at your disposal, the next step is to actively implement them in your life. This book is not only a source of information, but a guide to personal transformation. It encourages you to continue exploring, learning and growing.

Your reinvention is a continuous process, a journey without a final destination, and that is the wonderful thing about life. You will face obstacles and moments of doubt, and there will be days when the road seems uphill. However, it is in those moments that your resilience and determination will be most important.

Final Reflection

As we complete this journey of self-discovery and personal transformation, I invite you to pause and reflect on what you have learned. Consider how the concepts and tools explored in this book can be integrated into your daily life to foster a fuller, happier existence.

Ask yourself: What is the first step I will take to apply these learning's? How can I continue moving toward a life full of purpose and meaning? This moment of reflection not only closes a chapter, but opens the door to a future full of possibilities.

Remember that each new day represents an opportunity to grow and reinvent yourself. Stay focused on your purpose, celebrate small achievements, and face challenges with resilience and hope.

It's wonderful to know that you are committed to moving forward with the conviction that the path to happiness and personal fulfillment is a continuous journey! I am here to accompany you on this journey, so do not hesitate to connect with me through my social networks and my website frankiecotto.com, where you can find courses and other resources that will complement your transformation process. I am excited to support you and celebrate your successes.

You can do it!

NOTES

ABOUT THE AUTHOR

Frankie, a soul passionate about personal growth and genuine happiness, has dedicated his life to helping others discover their purpose and transform their lives. With a multifaceted career, he has transitioned from being a vice president at a banking institution to becoming a certified personal trainer, writer, speaker, and coach.

Along the way, Frankie has faced significant challenges that led him to redefine himself and find new opportunities in times of adversity. From opening a gym fueled by his passion for fitness to guiding others in their well-being through his books and lectures, his mission has always been to inspire and motivate those seeking a life full of meaning and joy.

With a unique perspective that blends science, spirituality, and life experience, Frankie offers practical tools and transformative strategies to achieve authentic happiness and personal reinvention. His empathetic approach and ability to connect with people at various stages of life have allowed many to follow his example and discover their own path to personal fulfillment.

As you explore the pages of this book, you will uncover the accumulated wisdom of years of experience and continuous learning, as well as the deep conviction that everyone—regardless of where they are in life—can reinvent themselves and live with purpose.

www.ingramcontent.com/pod-product-compliance
Lightning Source LLC
LaVergne TN
LVHW010919110826
845149LV00013B/2424